MW01602662

AN *extraordinary* LIFE

JOSEPHINE E. JONES

by *WENDY JONES*

Ida Bell Publishing, LLC
P. O. Box 175
Springfield, NJ 07081

www.idabellpublishing.com

idabellpub@gmail.com

© 2017 Wendy Jones

All rights reserved. No part of this book may be reproduced in
any form or by any electronic or mechanical means including
information storage and retrieval systems, without written permission
from the publisher. The only exception is by a reviewer,
who may quote short excerpts in a review.

Printed in the United States of America

This book is printed on sustainable paper.

Cover design and interior design by Natalie Marino / www.marinogallery.com

Cover photo from author's collection
Culinary Art photos by the late John Turner
All other photos from the author's collection

Copy editing and proofreading by Frank Steele / www.steele-editing.com

Library of Congress Control Number: 2017907552

Includes bibliographical references.

ISBN 978-1-9463-4802-9 (soft cover)

Wendy Jones:

This book is dedicated to the people who helped to shape the person that I have become

To all my fathers: Len Jones, Willie Simon, Calvin Henderson, James P. Ebaugh, Henry Weigl, Milton Kelly, Edwin M. Slote, Lawrence Duke, Gene, Lee Moody, Eddie, and Baker

To my mother: Josephine E. Jones
And to the other black women whose stories have yet to be told

Josephine E. Jones:

To my parents: Anna Nance Ebaugh and Scott Ebaugh

CONTENTS

NOTE TO READER

My mother's voice is the heart of this book about her life. Although the results of my interviews with my mother have been reorganized and edited, these are her words. The Relatives section consists of thumbnail sketches of family members who are an important part of my mother's life story. The Notes section provides historical context and supplementary material for the incidents and people she discusses. And finally, in the Appendix, I describe how my mother nurtured my education.

RELATIVES

Three of my mother's sisters

Vera, who has an innate sense of style, wears her beret at an angle and really does look French. On her long subway commutes, Vera devours one thick romance novel after another. The turbulent sea created by her decisions sends waves crashing into Mama's life for years.

Sally tries to figure out "whodunit" before finishing her Perry Mason novels. Sally's cap of curly black hair falls over her right eye as she throws her head back and laughs while holding a glass of scotch, murky with milk, in her right hand. Sally's love for my mother rescues Mama from a dangerous situation.

Nora buys the rhythm and blues hits as soon as they come out. She not only dances to the record player, Nora can also fix it and anything else that needs repair. At 18, she helps my mother by becoming, for a while, my long-term babysitter.

My mother's youngest brother

Calvin, my favorite uncle, gives all his sisters' children affectionate nicknames: One-Plait is mine. As he shaves with a straight razor, brush, and a mug of soapy lather, Calvin's male ritual mesmerizes me. Although his alcoholism saddens her, Mama cherishes Calvin.

My mother's nephews (Vera's oldest sons)

Ken, a fraternal twin from Vera's first marriage, and his minutes-younger brother **Ben** are professional butchers. With his slow smile, Ken is the quieter twin. Ken's care, when he becomes ill, is a source of tension between Mama and other family members.

Five of my mother's nieces and nephews (Vera's sons and daughter)

Ken and **Ben** (fraternal twins)

Steve

Nelson and **Nina** (fraternal twins)

PROLOGUE

CALLING FORTH MAMA'S VOICE

One early spring afternoon I found my mother sitting in the darkened dining room of her brownstone, dressed in black, head bent in depression. Despite the problems that had cascaded through our lives when Mama was raising me—my father leaving when I was an infant, my mother working three jobs to support us, Mama's siblings borrowing money they never repaid—I had never seen her depressed. When I asked what was wrong, my mother told me that it didn't seem that her life had come to much. I told her that wasn't true, but it did no good.

I had finished a play and had been looking for my next writing adventure. Here it was, staring me in the face. I told Mama that she had a story that would interest others.

In the 1960s, this sharecropper's daughter became, as far as I had been able to discover, the first black woman in management at a Fortune 500 company. The company was Standard Brands, which produced Chase & Sanborn Coffee, Royal Gelatin, and Planters Peanuts. It is now Kraft Heinz.

My mother also raised me as a single parent working six, and sometimes seven, days a week so that I could go to private schools and later to Yale and Columbia. In addition, Mama was a community activist in Harlem, encouraging young people and helping to restore a formerly drug-saturated block.

Why was education so important to her? How did my mother's attitude toward education affect my life? How did she come to be the person she became?

Her life was directly affected by the Great Migration, the civil rights movement, the women's movement, the gentrification of Harlem, and the AIDS epidemic. Mama's story was an American story, a Great Migration story, a New York story, a black family's story, a mother-daughter story, and the story of a woman's fight for creativity in the workplace.

Not only the circumstances of her individual life but also policies, laws, and practices specifically targeting black Americans and black women had opposed her.

Mama had triumphed over all these obstacles. Hers was a life story worth telling.

My mother was born to Anna Nance and Scott Ebaugh in 1920, in Cross Hill, South Carolina, on two borders of human time: near the end of the month and early in the morning, before daylight. And there was one more border: the border between life and death. Because Mama was a breech birth, Big Ma almost died. From the moment of her birth, my mother insisted on doing things her way. This approach to the world would continue throughout her life.

In addition to the colored midwife already present, a white doctor was called. This was clearly an emergency, but why would a white doctor deliver the baby of a black sharecropper in 1920 in South Carolina? When I asked Mama about this, she said, "People thought a lot of my daddy." When the doctor asked Big Pa which one he should save, his wife or the baby, my grandfather answered, "Save them both." Big Ma and Big Pa in their name choices connected her to both family and community. Josephine Willie Beatrice was named after her father's mother, her mother's brother, and the midwife. Mama was the fifth child and the fourth daughter born alive. By the time the family was complete, she would be one of nine children—seven girls and two boys.

When the doctor had done as requested, perhaps some sleep-deprived friend or family member, since Big Pa was illiterate, wrote my mother's name and birth date in the family Bible by the light of the kerosene lamp.

At the age of twenty, she found out the date was wrong. The doctor had compounded the error by listing her birth date as the day he filed the papers. This mistake landed Mama's birthday in the following month. It became her legal birthday.

Whenever I'm doing business on my mother's behalf, bank and government employees look at me with suspicion when it takes me a beat to give this legal fiction as Mama's date of birth.

As Mama tells this story, she's smiling. She is particularly gleeful that this mistake meant she was able to work an extra month before being legally declared sixty-five, the traditional retirement age when she was working. It was just like my mother to rejoice in a longer working life. She was fortunate, for most of her life, to have had work that she loved.

Sitting down to tape Mama's story, I tell her to begin at the beginning and imagine that her grandchildren are listening.

CHAPTER 1

FARMING WITH FATHER

Emerging as a superpower after World War I, the United States was a country of 106 million people in 1920. For the first time, the nation had more people living in cities than on farms or in small towns. Eight million Model T's were scaring horses and buggies off the dirt roads. At the same time, all white women and black women in the North—25 percent of the three million black women eligible to vote—had won the right to vote in 1919 with the Nineteenth Amendment. In 1920—despite active opposition from most white suffragettes during the 70-year battle for enfranchisement—Northern African American women cast their first votes in a national election.

The year of my mother's birth was bracketed by horrible events of racially motivated violence toward black people. The summer before—1919, dubbed "the red summer" by the African American writer James Weldon Johnson—was the scene of white-initiated race riots in 26 cities in both the North and the South, including New York City, Chicago, Illinois; Elaine, Arkansas; Washington, DC; and Charleston, South Carolina. In 1921, a white mob in Tulsa, Oklahoma, set fire to and totally destroyed the black neighborhood of Greenwood—known as the Black Wall Street for its superb business district—killing 300 people.

There was happier news in 1920 in the world of popular music. The black singer Mamie Smith made the first blues record with the word "blues" in the title, "Crazy Blues."

Cross Hill, South Carolina, where Mama was born in 1920, was near the path the Cherokee used to reach the fish dams on the Savannah River before the Europeans came. Laurens County, where the village is located, is in the Piedmont area of South Carolina. This northwestern corner of the state receives its name from its location at the foothills of the Blue Ridge Mountains.

Despite what most of us have heard about the 1920s, there were no flappers flapping in Cross Hill. At that time, Laurens County had over 42,000 residents, about 60 percent of whom were black. Most people earned their living either growing cotton or turning it *into fabric in the textile mills. My mother grew up using kerosene lamps, which cast their glow on walls covered with newspapers and pictures from the Sears catalog. Her family had created this "wallpaper" to brighten up the cabin that was their home. That day in April, Mama began her story.*

The first thing I remember was when my father went away in 1922. I remember watching and waiting for him to come home. He had gone away to work up in Buffalo, New York. It was a year when he was having a hard time with the farm. The boll weevils were eating up all the cotton, so he went up north. He started working at the headquarters of the Lackawanna Railroad Company. Pa laid crossties for the railroad, which started in New Jersey and ran all the way up through Lackawanna until it got to Buffalo.

The day he left, I went part of the way with him, as far as the mailbox. There he told me to go back. Pa had been gone a month or so before my family realized that I had stopped eating and playing. I just crawled into a shell.

When Mama took me to the doctor, he looked at me and asked where my father was. My mother told him that he'd gone north. The doctor told her that that's why I wasn't eating; I was emotionally sick. He told her the family would have to do things with me to get my mind off him. If she didn't, she would lose me. I was grieving myself to death.

Mama showed me the fall colors of the leaves and a running brook, where I saw a fish. When she showed me these things, it helped me get over my grief. She also told me that my father had just gone to work and he would be back. I thought maybe he was dead. When I knew he would be back, I got over my grief. In the meantime, we started getting letters from him. My mother would always read the letters to us.

It wasn't Christmas yet, but I know it was cold because we had a fire when Pa came back. He brought a lot of balloons and had something different for each of us. He gave me what we used to call a glass doll, but I guess it was a china doll. It was beautiful. Naturally, it was white. We didn't have black dolls then.

My sisters—especially my older sisters—kept telling me to get the doll so they could see it and play with it. They kept pushing and jumping around and kept me going back and getting it. This one wanted it and that one wanted it, until . . . it got broken that night!

Then they all said, "Oh, she doesn't have a doll now." I cried about it for three or four days. I got more dolls, but I didn't get that doll back. I realized then that they always wanted what I had and not what they had. Pa didn't do any more for me than he did for the rest of them, but he encouraged me. I saw how he did things, so I patterned my life after his.

When Pa left again, I crawled back into a shell. He was just home on vacation. I was three years old. That was 1923.

I don't know when my father came back home to stay. I guess it must have been about two years altogether that he worked on the railroad.

He had planned to go north and not come back because there wasn't anything on the farm for him. He was making good money in Buffalo. Pa had a good offer to bring his family there. The foreman in charge of the crew wanted my father to come—my father was the leader of the work gang—so he could make Pa a foreman, too.

The company wanted to turn the big house they had in Buffalo into a boardinghouse. My mother would take care of the men who worked on the railroad and we would live there.

But Mama was an only child, and she wouldn't leave her mother. She said it was too far away. My father told her she could always come back because he would be working for the railroad; the employees and their family rode the train for free. But she still didn't want to go, so Pa came back to the farm. My father said he couldn't live any longer without his family. We were living in Cross Hill, South Carolina, on Route 1 between Cross Hill and Chappells. This was still in Laurens County.

Right after my father and mother got married in January 1911—sometime between then and 1916—he worked in Greenville in some of the mills there. He didn't want to farm. Black men were porters in the mills; that's the only thing they were allowed to do, was low-level jobs. My mother never went to any white people's house to cook, wash, or iron. Even if he had to work on two or three jobs, Pa supported us, without my mother having to go to work.

Greenville was noted for its cotton mills. I don't know how many, but at least eight or nine, maybe more: Poinsett Mill, Union Bleachery . . .

They made cloth out of cotton after it had been picked and ginned. It was turned into cotton batts. Then cotton rows. Then it was sent to the factory where they made cloth out of it, dyed it, and printed it. Only whites were allowed to operate the dye and print machines.

That's why the poor white people in the Southern states had a level of education that was much lower than the poor blacks. Their kids came out of school at ten and twelve and went into the factory. The black children weren't allowed in the factories, so they went on to school. By the time most white children were fifteen years old, they had worked two years in the factory, both the boys and the girls. So being white was a disadvantage. They kept the blacks out of the factory, but they also handicapped the white children.

In 1916, Pa was not a sharecropper. When he came back to the farm from working in the mill, he bought himself a fast mule and rented land. The white owners of the property wanted him to sell the mule. Then he would have had to become a sharecropper. Because he wouldn't have his own livestock. He refused to sell.

We don't know how the house caught on fire. My mother had gone to my grandmother's to spend the night, and she took the children with her. There hadn't been any fire in the house all day, no one cooking. About four o'clock that afternoon the house went up in fire and smoke. Everything was lost except what my mother had on her back and the three children she had with her. That's how my father got behind. The children kept coming about every two years, so Pa was never able to get out from under that setback.

Eventually he did have to sell the mule to plant. This was May, the beginning of the planting season. He had to plant cotton and rent a house from somebody and come back to farm the land. Pa was sharecropping now.

Sharecropping means that for every dollar you make, you give the owner, usually a white man, one dollar. You did all the work and the owner furnished the land, the animals, the seeds, and the guano; that's bird droppings we used as fertilizer. You bought the groceries from the company store. Sometimes the prices were higher than elsewhere and sometimes they weren't.

My father was always a lucky person. People knew he meant what he said, that he had a good character, and was responsible. Basically, we didn't have any trouble. My father got whatever he needed.

If you were renting, you'd just say, "Well, I'll give you three bales of cotton for renting this land." But you made thirty bales of cotton total, so the rest was yours. There were three categories: owning, renting, and sharecropping. Sharecropping was the most dependent category. As a sharecropper, you were least likely to be able to buy your own land.

I don't think he was cheated within the system. But if you're giving somebody half of what you make, there is no way you can get ahead.

In the thirties, during Hoover's time, the government had a program to get the farmland back in production. If you had a son (he had to be twenty-one), they'd give you so many acres of land and a house. You would pay the government so much back in cotton, but you'd become the owner of this property.

My eldest brother said he wasn't going to be around. So we didn't have anyone to sign up to get this farmland. At that time we were living maybe ten miles out from Gray Court near Route 1.

In my early remembrance of farming, I was running behind my father. By the time I was five years old, I was getting up early so I could go to the field with him. I wanted to ride the mule. He was usually up at four o'clock in the morning to get his breakfast: bacon, molasses, and bread. My oldest sister would get up and make breakfast. Then he went to the field.

If I didn't go to the field, I was there in time to ride the mule back at twelve o'clock. But usually I took him water around ten o'clock. Then I stayed in the field until noontime, so I could ride the mule back to the house. I don't know what was fascinating about riding the mule— now I'm afraid of them.

To let us know it was noon, the white owner of the land in the big house—which we weren't allowed to go into—rang a bell. Another way to tell it was noontime was when your shadow stood up beneath you.

When I came back at noon riding the mule, I was coming in for dinner. We called the midday meal dinner. We cooked string beans or peas and had meat that was cooked in a pot. We'd have some bread, rice, or potatoes along with these vegetables. We usually had to have something sweet because my father always had to have dessert. We'd make some kind of pie: apple, peach, or sweet potato.

We had a bench around the fireplace where we sat and ate. We would sit there and listen to stories that Mother and Dad would tell before we went to bed. The bench was long enough for five of us to sit on. But the others always pushed me off the end. Then I would cry.

Dad finally eliminated that. He cut a block off a tree for me to sit on, like a stool. They couldn't push me off of that.

When I was five, the oldest sister, who was 14, did the cooking. We used to have to take turns. One sister cooked one week and one took care of the wash one week. All of us had to take care of our own beds. We had to do the dishes after we got big enough to do them. The girls took turns making the boys' beds. The boys didn't do anything in the house. Oh, they dirtied it up, but they didn't clean anything.

Pa cooked Sunday dinner with Ma. He was born late in his mother's life, so he was the only child left at home. His mother taught him to do housework to help her around the house. He even taught me how to embroider.

My brothers would cut the wood and bring it in for the stove, for the fire to heat up the water. They would go get water when we had to go to the spring to get it. When we'd drawn it out of the well in the yard, they might bring it into the house. And they would get water if they wanted some and there wasn't any in the house. The boys had to work in the field, but they did the bare minimum. Any extra work that was needed, my father did it.

You planted the cotton seeds in May, and then they came up. The plants got about two inches tall. After that, they had to be thinned. You planted them thick in order to get enough, because not all of them would come up. In each hole there had to be a stalk of cotton. Eventually they did make a mechanical planter that dropped every other one, so we didn't have to plant it so thick. You still had to go out there and hold it, work the soil, and build the dirt around it so it could grow. The plow couldn't get that close. If it did, the plow would cut the plant.

The cotton plant was on a row. The field was divided into what they called terraces. You built a high bed so the water couldn't wash it down. You could jump over it, just like this balcony up here on my house.

You planted in May and worked it in June. Usually there was just a month where it grew. By July, you'd finished working the soil, and it had to grow and develop. The plant became a bloom, and then it became a cotton bud, like an acorn. Then the flower dropped off and the bud got ripe, opened up, and made the cotton. There were five little bolls in there. You put your fingers in there and you pulled it out. The seeds were in the cotton. That is what you had to take to the gin.

The gin separated the seeds from the cotton. Thirteen hundred pounds of cotton with the seeds and the debris in it became five hundred pounds after it was ginned.

The farms that we stayed on usually had their own gin. I don't know whether we gave them bales of cotton in payment or whether we gave them some of the seeds.

Usually about the last of August, it was time to start picking the cotton. By the end of October, before Thanksgiving, you wanted to finish picking all the cotton because it'd gotten ripe. It was still warm. If you weren't finished before Thanksgiving, you had to keep on until you were finished. If you didn't, the frost would kill it.

In March, my father started to get the soil ready for the planting. You had to cultivate the soil; you had to turn it over. You see, it had been lying dormant all winter. It had rained on it, snowed on it. Sometimes he and my brothers would go clean out the stables and scatter manure over it, so the soil would get fertilizer.

By May, he was ready to plant. April was too early. It was not quite warm enough. Around the last of May and the first of June, we'd start hoeing. And the cycle started again.

The weather and the boll weevil were the enemies of the crop. The boll weevil was a bug that would eat the cotton up. It ate the cotton after the boll came on it and punctured it, usually before it could get a chance to open up. If it did open, maybe there would be two or three bolls instead of five. These bolls, little balls of cotton, looked like hickory nuts. The first year the boll weevil came was 1922 or 1923.

The farmers hadn't developed a poison for it then. Later they did develop some kind of pesticide. You put molasses in this powder, mixed it together, and made a mop out of an old piece of cloth. You put this on a handle and spread it on the plants, and it would kill the boll weevil.

The early frost . . . if it came, the cotton was finished then. In the summer, a drought or too much water could destroy the cotton. If you got too much rain, the cotton would grow, but it wouldn't develop. It just kept growing, growing, growing. Not enough flowers developed. It was not hot enough for the bees to come. The bees are the ones that pollinate all flowers to make them develop, including the cotton.

In 1932, there wasn't any frost and the cotton repeated itself on the same stalk. We saved two rows to see if it could produce another crop, and it did. The change in seasons didn't occur, so the cotton lived.

From Thanksgiving until the first of March, you really didn't do anything on the farm. Everything had gone into hibernation. That's why we could be in school during those months. By that time, the vegetables had been canned.

Pa had a garden where we raised our own vegetables. He had the most beautiful vegetables and watermelons, and plenty of them. They didn't rot in the field and he didn't sell them all. He let neighbors come get what they wanted. If it was a good crop year, there would be such an abundance of fruit and vegetables, you couldn't can them all. You had canned tomatoes, string beans, okra, and corn. Everything was canned so we could have it during the winter.

You always had potatoes. The potatoes were plowed up, and you kept them the year round. You banked them by making a tent of corn husks, straw, and dirt and putting a hole in it for the potatoes. You got them out and ate them when you got ready.

We also made watermelon-rind preserves and pickles. With tomatoes, we sometimes made something called chow chow. That's like a relish with red peppers, green cabbage, and green tomatoes in it. We pickled green tomatoes, too.

We ate the chow chow on vegetables. We grew our own beans: pinto beans, black-eyed peas, field peas, and we had a pea that we called a crowder pea that today is called a chickpea.

The collard greens and turnip greens lasted through the winter. We also made pickled beets, preserves, and jellies out of all the berries nearby. Basically, you had stuff for the winter.

I don't know why all of a sudden you have to revert to this commercial canned food, when you can get fresh food and can it.

We ate a lot of fruit in the South. I don't know why people in the South don't eat more of it now. During the summer, blackberries grew wild. We canned blackberries—we made jelly out of them; we made jam.

We cooked them and made wine and canned them for pies.

Peach trees were also around. We would cut the peaches up, dry them, and put them on top of a piece of white material made out of a flour sack. Then we put them on the tin roof of the barn or on the roof of the house. We would lay them on that and let them dry. They were now dried peaches.

We made fruit pies out of those and called them flapjacks or applejacks; we made applesauce. All kinds of preserves were made out of fruit and canned galore. You can can apples and dry them, too.

I don't understand why there is nothing but peach cobbler in black Southern cuisine restaurants. We made a peach cobbler, but the peach cobbler was not the main Southern dish. The potato custard was the main dessert, as well as pound cake. Black Southerners made cakes and pies. They made all kinds of cakes: the coconut cake, the chocolate cake, and the pound cake. Cakes were mostly what you would find at any gathering anywhere you went or at any home.

You made corn meal out of the corn and you also made grits out of it and what you call the hominy. That is, you cook the dry corn and it becomes hominy. It's the whole grain of the corn. It's swollen and it's been husked.

We can take the basic Southern recipes and redo them to make a new style of soul food cookbook. We can use the same ingredients, but use them lightly. There's nothing to do with the ham bones but boil them, then put them in the refrigerator and take the fat off. You still have the same taste, but you've eliminated the fat.

I think the relatives on my father's side had strokes from eating too much salt and from having too much fat in the diet. You got the sausage, you got the fatback, you got the ham, and all that stuff is full of fat; and the chicken is fried, so it's full of fat. That's why I don't eat that stuff. Everything is fat.

I think high blood pressure comes from emotions, too. Most anybody who dies with a stroke does have high blood pressure.

We always killed the pigs that we raised. Sometimes the meat was enough to last through the winter and sometimes it wasn't, according to how many folks came by the house. I never knew our house, on a Sunday, when we were growing up, when there weren't at least four or five extra people for dinner. They'd eat and we'd have to cook more. And we always had chickens. When we lived near the river, Papa would also put in a basket to catch fish.

My father always had some money around, because in the wintertime he'd cut a lot of wood to sell in the town and he would do odd jobs around the white people's house. He was the butcher in the area where we lived, so we had a lot of extra meat around. The upper-class white people did not eat chitterlings (pig's large intestines), the smalls (pig's small intestines), the liver, the lights (pancreas), hog's head, and pig's feet. They gave my father what they did not eat as his pay for killing this pig.

Pa received all the byproducts of the pig: the liver, the lights, the chitterlings, the smalls. You can take the toenails and make a tea. You can eat everything from the pig except his hair. And you can take that and make brushes out of it.

I guess that is why I know how to survive. You do what you have to do. I don't want to struggle or deny myself anything. That life is behind me!

We always had enough to eat in the winter. The only thing we had to buy was sugar. We didn't have a refinery to make the sugar from the sugar cane. Not too far from us, they had a molasses mill, and I think you got one gallon out of the five. The miller took the rest as payment for using the mill. The machinery in the mill went around and around. In one place, the juice came out and in the next place it was cooking. It was hot. I doubt if any of my siblings had ever been to the mill. All these things I went with my father to see.

That's how I got to go to the sawmill, to see the logs being pushed through, the lumber being made, turned into planks. It always fascinated me. There again, the mules pulled this thing around. They didn't have the electrical motors and mechanical motors that they have now.

The place where the corn was made into grits and meal was a water mill. The water turned the wheel over; it was on a creek. These were the things that I saw firsthand.

After World War I, a lot of people left the Southern states and came north to work in the meat industry in Chicago, the factories here in New York, and the automobile factories in Detroit. Wherever the train was headed, that was where they went.

Some of these men left and they never came back. My father always saw about those widows and those children. He would tell them how to plant and what to do. I guess that is why I was always reaching out to people.

CHAPTER 2

GETTING AN EDUCATION

While high school graduation in 1940 was difficult for Americans as a whole—the 1940 census reveals that over 50 percent of all Americans went no further than the eighth grade in school—for colored people in the rural South, it was nearly impossible. High schools were located in the cities, not in the rural areas where most blacks lived. Although the population of black and white teenagers in South Carolina was roughly equal, their high school enrollment numbers were not. White high school enrollment in the 1933–1934 school year was 60 percent, but black high school enrollment in that same year, the year Mama should have started high school, was only 12 percent.

The national standard high school went to the 12th grade, but 90 percent of African Americans lived in the

South where the school boards mandated that schools end in the 11th grade. The county training schools were designed to train black students to teach elementary school. Only after Southern states began requiring college degrees for teacher certification did 12th grade high schools become the norm.

The next thing I remember clearly is wanting to follow my sisters and brothers to school. But they said they couldn't take me because I walked too slowly. My father couldn't take me to school because he was selling cordwood to people in the village. So I didn't get to go.

I started asking for books and papers. I wanted to read. I wanted to write. Everybody else was going, and I didn't understand what they were doing. I don't know what kind of books they got me, but we got books. And we always had a newspaper around the house.

I don't remember us having the ABC blocks, but somebody had written the ABC's down, so I printed them on another piece of paper. Then I started asking, "Well, how is this going to become a word?"

My father, though he could not read, had some kind of understanding, that you put the letters together and they would spell words. I said, "I want to read." Then we got the books. I knew the ABC's, so I could spell the word out, but I didn't know the meaning of it. I would spell the word, then I would cry until somebody pronounced it for me.

The first word I remember was "the." That was when I started getting the sounds of the letters, the "T" and the "H" and the "E." That was how I learned how to read. I would spell the words and sound it out. The family couldn't understand why I wanted to read, but I wanted to know what was going on, what was in this print.

I wanted to know what was that story about in the newspaper or the magazine. I would get one word, then I wanted to know another word. I wanted to read the whole book!

Mother was a great reader, but maybe there were too many of us, that it took too much out of her. Or maybe I annoyed her so until she just didn't have the patience to deal with it.

I learned how to read before I went to school. I didn't go to school until I was eight years old, and that was a year late, but I was already reading, writing, counting, and making up sentences before I went to school.

I didn't stay in the first grade that long because I already knew what they were teaching. In the places where we lived, the school was a long ways to walk. My siblings weren't interested in school, because sometimes they didn't go themselves. That made a difference. When we moved close to school, I didn't have any problem, because my father would take me if they didn't go.

They didn't send you to school until you were seven years old. I don't know whether it was the same for whites or it was just for blacks. At seven years old, you were already half grown. I guess that's why a lot of people in the South did not get an education or did not finish school, because they started too late. At seven, if you didn't have anybody supporting you at home, if you hadn't been pushing and struggling like I had been, what would you know?

After my father saw that I was determined to go to school, he was 100 percent behind me. We had our books and things to wear.

When I was in second grade, we had spelling bees. The word was "strength." Whoever missed a day had to go to the end of the line. I had missed one day. I don't think I was sick, because I would fight to go to school. "Strength" came all the way down the line. Nobody else could spell it. I spelled it and went to the head of the line. But I still got punished.

I fault my mother today. I swore if I ever had a child and anything ever happened at school, I would go to the school to defend my child and see what had happened.

The teacher excused the class and told them that she was going to give me a whipping. She said I wasn't absent; I must have cheated. She didn't know how I could be at the head of the line if I had been absent. But I had spelled the word!

The other students in the class said, "Josephine wasn't here yesterday. She was at the end of the line when class started today. Look at your roll book. She wasn't here yesterday." But she wouldn't listen.

I found out later that my oldest sister and the teacher were talking to the same young man, and the teacher took it out on me.

I just wanted Mama to go say something to her to let her know that she was wrong. But my mother wouldn't go, so . . . She just said, what could she do? It was already done.

The teacher hit me on the leg and cut it, and blood came out of it. I didn't tell my father, because I think he probably would have gone there and choked her. Mama didn't tell Daddy about it either.

We didn't go to school nine months straight. We had about six or seven months of school broken up between seasons of farming. We didn't start school until the last of September, and then it was over in May. If the farming was going, sometimes you didn't start until the last of October so you'd be out to get the cotton picked.

Sometimes the ones who weren't old enough to pick went to school, and the older ones who had to pick stayed at home. We usually had about a month of summer school in July and August when there was no farming. There were times when we went a half a day on a Saturday, too. This is what everybody in the area did.

Our school was a little different. It was called Laurens County Training School. Julius Rosenwald's Foundation was the one that built the schools in that area. The white people had a brick school and we had a plank school. The white people wouldn't let him build ours out of the same material. His picture hung on the school wall, and Abraham Lincoln's picture was in our chapel. I think Rosenwald came out of Chicago. I know he was Jewish. His foundation built the schools for the blacks throughout the Southern states. The average white American did not want the blacks to have that much of an education, so we had a one-room schoolhouse.

We changed classes. There were about seven or eight teachers there and we had a principal who was a great guy, a very hard disciplinarian, especially on the young black men. His name was Mr. Louis Charles Jamison. He was half-white. I think he came from Anderson, South Carolina.

When he found out I was determined to get an education—there were eight of us children then—he asked my mother if I could go to Laurens city during the week and stay with his mother. The school there was still an all-black school, but it was a better school. They went to school from September to May straight through. He was an only child and his mother lived alone. He asked Mama if I could go to Laurens during the week, stay with his mother so I could be company for her, and go to school there.

Mr. Jamison said if there was one in the family to be educated, I should be the one, because I had great potential. "I just want to help you help her, and you'd help me too, because I don't want Mother there alone. I know your family. And I know she would be a nice child for my mother to have. I'd go to Laurens and get her on Friday evening. I would come Sunday evening and take her back. I wouldn't want you to do without her on the weekends."

He boarded there in Gray Court during the week. Mr. Jamison said he and his mother would take care of me and buy all my clothes, and do everything for me.

My mother said no, I couldn't go, because she wanted the same thing for all her children. If Mama had let me go, I would have finished high school on time. He would have sent me to college. His mother looked as if she was white. They had resources. He wasn't married then. Eventually, in his late 30s, he did get married to a woman as light-skinned as he was.

I wanted to learn languages, travel, and move ahead. I had already visualized myself in France, in Paris. My oldest brother told us about France when we were little. It was day in France when it was night here. I wanted to see that, to cross the Atlantic Ocean solo like Lindbergh. I thought that what anybody else could do—we could do. But that opportunity was very quickly nipped in the bud.

When we went to school, sometimes we didn't have the right books or hadn't been able to get the right shoes. One year we didn't get to go to school that much. I was in the fourth grade. I was ten. My sister Vera and I didn't pass, because you had to have a certain number of days in school.

I always took Vera through school with me. Vera is my mother's fourth child; she was twelve at the time. I am the fifth child. She was never interested in school. But I knew I had to help her so I could keep going. I'd do my lessons, then I'd drill her until she had hers memorized.

Then when we got ready to go back to school in the summer, I told Mother to tell the principal to let us go into the fifth grade. I was already too old and I didn't want to be back there with those other children. She said no, she wasn't going to school, and it would be all right.

I went to school early one morning and asked Mr. Jamison could we try the fifth grade, that I knew the work.

He said, "Let me look at your record. Yes, you did well, but the problem is you didn't come to school."

I told him we hadn't come to school because we had to work on the farm.

He said, "Well, all right, go ahead. I'll tell your teacher to put you in the fifth grade."

So I went to the fifth grade and I did well. Vera did well, too.

In the sixth grade, we had what they called field day. We went down to Clinton, South Carolina, to Bell Street. Sally, who was the baby at the time, was five years old. Sally and I were the ones who most excelled in the academic area. My older sister stopped going to school, and then the second oldest sister stopped. Then my oldest brother stopped, too.

When Sally and I went down to Bell Street, I made her a coat out of one of my grandma's old coats, a pretty brown coat. It was old-fashioned, with a belt around it and a shirred waist. It was big, so there was enough material to make her a coat and a tam. We rode down on a flatbed truck to participate in this program.

I was seven when Sally was born. She was Mama's eighth child. Ma was tired of babies, and I was reliable. I didn't like dolls; they couldn't talk. Ever since Sally could talk, I had taught her what I knew. She could spell and sound out words. I took her to school with me when she was four years old. When she was five years old, she was in first grade. The teachers didn't care as long as she sat down and listened.

Sally won first prize in the group she was in and I won second prize. Our field day was sports and recitations. I did current events and she did some readings, but I don't remember exactly what they were.

Several of the students, who had gone away to college down to Benedict, heard the news and they wrote to the principal of our school, Mr. Jamison, to congratulate my sister and me on winning our awards.

My family didn't seem to care anything about us winning. They acted as if it was something that everybody was capable of doing. I think my father was proud of us. He would always tell you, "That was good, that was great." But in the beginning, what you're looking for is a warm welcome from all the family. My siblings just didn't acknowledge it.

That is why I knew when I had a child that I had to give that child all the support he or she needed. If I had had the support I needed, I wouldn't have been going back to school at forty-four to get a certificate from the New York Institute of Dietetics.

My family felt there was something wrong with me because I was a bookworm. I didn't care about toys or dolls. I could do without eating to get a book! I always knew there was a better way of making a living. You were going to have to have an education. I think you can educate yourself, but you have to have those avenues opened.

If I could have gotten the siblings—maybe just the five of us, which were four girls and one boy—to do something together, we could have done wonders with our lives.

I wanted us to have a family business. First, I thought we could be a group, something like the Jackson Five became. We could have learned how to sing. We could have learned how to do a play together. All these things I tried to get them to do, but nobody would ever cooperate. I saw no reason why somebody couldn't sing, somebody else couldn't dance, and somebody else couldn't play the piano.

The five of us played together, ate together, slept together. We called ourselves the Five Troopers. In birth order that would be Vera, then myself, Calvin, Maude, then Sally. We were all two years apart, except for Sally.

There are three years between her and Maude. Sally was the last sibling in the family for about eight years. That's when the last one of us was born, Nora. The name Ebaugh was something that I wanted to be highlighted. Whatever we were doing, our father would have been there to encourage us.

In 1929 I was nine years old and in the fourth grade. I had English, math, and history. We arrived at school at 8:30 a.m. in the morning, and had reading, writing, spelling, and English. The afternoon was usually dedicated to homemaking. We had an hour for cooking and an hour for sewing.

We had to make the costumes for the plays we called fairy tales. They were made out of crepe paper most of the time. Sometimes we might use cheap materials for the boys' costumes, but all girls' costumes were made out of crepe paper. We gathered the paper and sewed it on to an underskirt.

Sometimes it was a costume for an angel. We made wings out of wire and covered it with the crepe paper. Suppose you had to make a halo. You made it out of crepe paper, too. So you had all the spring colors, which made it very beautiful.

From fourth grade on, the girls took homemaking while the boys took shop and agriculture. At the end of the school term, our garments were put on display and we had a show with judges. One year, I won first prize for one of the dresses that I made.

I went to seventh grade in that school. I'd finished the seventh and was promoted to the eighth. High school started in eighth grade and went to the 11th. The graduating class of 1943 was the last 11th grade graduation. They skipped 1944. The board of education was upgrading our educational system. That meant we would start high school in the ninth grade instead of in the eighth grade.

This was 1935 and I was 15 years old. My last sibling, Nora, had just been born. That's when we moved up around Simpsonville. We lived far away from the school I finished seventh grade in. That was when my education began to be interrupted.

Although my father paid taxes, there were no buses for blacks, only for whites. The only way you could go to high school was to stay with some people in the neighborhood. So in 1936, Vera and I went to stay with Aunt Clara, Mama's stepsister, in Greenville to go to school. We didn't get to Aunt Clara's until January, so we had to repeat the seventh grade. We were promoted to the eighth grade again and we would've gone to Sterling High School, but we moved again.

The school in Cashville, where we moved, ran to eighth grade. We went to eighth grade in that school, but they wouldn't accept the credits in Greenville. Once again, we didn't get to go to school in Greenville until January, after the cotton was finished. Vera didn't try to get back into school; she went to work.

The principal wouldn't take me into the eighth grade. He said it was the beginning of the second semester and I wouldn't pass. I came back home and talked to my aunt about it. I was upset. She said, "Let's see what Mama Young can do."

Everybody looked up to her as a mother figure in the neighborhood. That was 1939; I guess she was in her fifties then.

The principal, Mr. Durant, was a member of Mama Young's church, Springfield Baptist. She told him that he should put me in the eighth grade, because I should have an education. And she was sure that I could catch up on the work. I went back to school the next day.

So I repeated both seventh and eighth grade, going twice through no fault of my own. We moved every two or three years. We would go to an area where the farming was more suitable. Very few areas in the country had high schools. You had to go to Spartanburg, Woodruff, Greenville, Fountain Inn, or Simpsonville. That's where the high schools were. We were always situated about 15 or 18 miles from these cities. I finally ended up staying alone in Greenville with Aunt Clara.

While I was fighting the battle to complete my education, my father was with me. He told me I could do anything I wanted to do, go anywhere I wanted to go.

The conflict there was that my siblings didn't want me to go to school. They said they were taking care of me while I was going to school and I wasn't doing any work. That was why I couldn't leave the farm to go to school when we were picking cotton. But my father should have just said I was going and sent me on. That was why I went to live with Aunt Clara.

My aunt took in washing and ironing. I helped her with that to pay my room and board. I bought my own food and paid her a dollar and a half a week to stay with her. When I came home, I helped her to do the laundry. That was my first year there.

The year after that, I got an evening job. I went to work from four until after dinner. I made dinner around six for a couple with a little baby. The husband worked at Union Bleachery at the mill.

The mills always furnished their people with living quarters. The person I worked for was Mr. Hall. The wife didn't work. He was one of the supervisors at the mill; I know because he dressed in a suit.

I usually got home around 7:30, then I would get my homework. If my aunt was behind in her work, I would help her with the laundry. After that, I would get ready for school the next day.

This is also the year I started working in the cafeteria at school. The government had a project they called the NYA, the National Youth Administration. Children in high school could work during the lunch hour or after school. But I preferred working during the lunch hour. At first I worked in the cooking area. I did the preparation of the foods, like making the hamburgers, cleaning the vegetables, and serving up the plates.

I'm not too sure whether you paid for your lunch or not. We didn't pay because we worked in the cafeteria. I have a feeling that there was a small fee, because everybody didn't eat. That was in ninth grade in 1940.

I would save some money and buy whatever I needed to wear. That was when I first opened my little savings account. The NYA paid six dollars a month. There was no job there in the summer, so in the summer I went home to help on the farm.

In tenth grade, I didn't work for that same lady. I had a lot of part-time jobs so I wouldn't have to do all that washing and ironing with my aunt. In the eleventh grade, I didn't work. I just helped my aunt with the laundry.

In my tenth and eleventh year, the cafeteria had a store, a commissary. I guess you couldn't do it now, but they sold candy and potato chips. So I didn't have to work back in the kitchen. It was in the shop basement, where the young men did the carpentry work.

I'd come back and go to school after I finished working on the farm. But after the first year, my father would let me come back in September when school started. If they got behind, I'd go stay a couple of days. Usually, I'd try to make it around holiday time so I wouldn't lose too many days out of school. I bought my own clothes and books with my own money.

I had problems when I got into eighth grade. I was so far advanced over the other students. The teacher didn't know that I had already gone through all this. In the homemaking class, we had to make an apron and we had to make what they call a tote bag now, which we called a carrying bag. You bought the handles from the five and ten-cent store, but you had to sew the rest of it by hand. The apron had to be made on the sewing machine at the school.

Because mine was so much neater than the rest, the teacher said that an adult, my aunt or somebody did it. My aunt had a machine, but it didn't even work! I never could make the teacher understand . . . That's why it's so hard for me now to accept it when somebody says I didn't do something. It's very difficult. These are the things that happen when you're a child and you can't defend yourself. I couldn't get her to understand that I had been making my clothes since I was twelve years old, so I sewed very well. In the end, she wouldn't give me an A. It was an A job, but she gave me a B.

If you didn't belong to a certain class, I don't care how well you did, you didn't get that top grade. They would always try to give light-skinned children the best grades, whether they made them or they didn't.

Most of the teachers themselves were light-skinned. One of the teachers that I was very grateful for was of my color. She, too, had had to work very hard because she was not of the light class. Then it was a thing in the South—I don't know what it was here in the North, but the lighter you were, you got more done for you . . . by blacks.

But I survived it. I think it made me stronger in a lot of ways. But it did hurt. I think there are a lot of people in prison for crimes that they didn't commit. Who's right and who's wrong? If the jury says you're wrong, you're wrong.

Sue Ellen Fields was the organist at Mount Olive Baptist Church and the director of our glee club. I sang in the glee club. We'd go to churches and to the air base. We sang in the school and at our graduation.

Graduation was one of the highlights of my life. I guess the thing I was most grateful for was that my father, my mother, and my aunt were there. I think all my sisters and brothers except my second sister and my oldest brother were there, too. We didn't have a party. My family came up from the country that night. I stayed and went back down to the country, Woodruff, South Carolina, after the next day or two.

I was the first in our family to graduate from high school. I graduated in 1943 in May; I turned 23 later that year.

We didn't get rings or pins, because we graduated during the war and they were saving all the metal for the war effort. But I was one of the holy ten. They called us that because we had the highest averages in the class. I received A's or B's in all of my subjects. We were entitled to scholarships for college. But I didn't know how to go about getting the scholarship, so I didn't get to take advantage of that.

That was another reason that I always said that if I ever became a parent that I would follow through to the bitter end to see that my child got a good education and that she got the things that were there for her.

But I don't hold my not understanding how to apply for the college scholarship against my parents, because they didn't know. I think it should have come from the school. But they didn't give the dark-skinned people too much help.

It did pay off as an adult in adult education. Everybody said, "Well, you have to get your GED." I said, "No, I got mine. I don't need a GED. I got my high school diploma!"

I was not going to work on a farm in that sun, but there were very few things open to us, except teaching and nursing. I'd tell my sister, Vera, something once and then she didn't know it. I didn't have enough patience for her to take three or four hours to absorb it. So I knew I couldn't teach. I thought once I'd go into nurse training. You could get free training in the WACs (Women's Army Corps), but somehow it wasn't what I really wanted.

I knew I wanted to do creative work. But we were limited to what we had in classes. I do believe I would have ended up in politics. Maybe I would have taken political science courses. I always felt as if I could change a lot of things that were being done, especially for the black race. We needed enough blacks there to tell them what we needed. Maybe I would have been a lawyer.

I think I would have liked to have been someone like Sojourner Truth or Harriet Tubman, or Ida B. Wells or Mary McLeod-Bethune. These were the black women that we were taught something about. Ever since I can remember, in February, around Abraham Lincoln's birthday, we had Negro History Week. That was when we talked about George Washington Carver, Booker T. Washington, W. E. B. DuBois, and Frederick Douglass; those are the names that come to my mind.

I think I did have something similar to them, something I could give to people. I ended up making people happy with food.

After graduation, I stayed around Woodruff for a while, and then I got a call from Greenville. This was Mrs. Stetson. She had a little girl named Rita. So I went to work for her as a cook. A young man came in to do the cleaning. That still wasn't what I wanted to do, but it was better than working on the farm.

I'd taken a test and passed the civil-service exam to be a clerk, but there were no clerk jobs in Greenville for black people. If I went to Washington, I'd be able to get a job. We had a cousin in Washington who was about my age; I could stay with her.

I said, "I'll have to leave South Carolina." In those days in high school in the South, you were really not prepared to do anything unless you went further, because they didn't have what were called trade schools there.

While I was planning to leave, my father had a stroke. He had it in 1943 in the fall, just after I graduated. He told me wherever I went to save my money. My father told me to get a round-trip ticket so I could come back home if things didn't work out.

I worked almost two years in Greenville, but then I decided I had to leave. I went back to Woodruff and talked to my father and he agreed, but I could see him weakening. I'd planned to leave on the first of December for Washington.

After I saw he was getting worse, I said, "I better stay, because with what little money I have, if I get to Washington and I don't have a job and have to come right back . . ." So I made up my mind to stay until after Christmas. This was 1945.

During this time he still thought I was going to Washington, DC, so he was telling me what to do and what not to do for the family. He saw that he was not getting any better. He was limping, but he could still walk. It was a warm December. We would walk and he would talk.

He didn't have any money to leave us, but he said if I promised to take care of my mother and my baby sister, Nora—he would always be around. There would be a way made for me.

I said, "I'll do the best I can, but you're not going anyplace. You're going to stay with us until I go to Washington and come back. You'll be here."

"I don't know about that, but I do have a lot of confidence—a lot of faith—that you'll do all right." This was the beginning of December.

On December 18, after midnight, I was making some curtains for the kitchen. I always made curtains for the whole house.

My father said to me, "Get Sally to help you."

"She's asleep." Everybody was in bed but me. "She's not going to do anything anyway."

"I don't know what's going to happen to that child. She seems to be the only one that really doesn't want to do any work. She doesn't want to help herself."

"That's all right. I'll get these finished."

He was in bed and he turned over. Then I heard this funny sound: woo hoo woo hoo.

I jumped up and said, "Daddy! Daddy!" He couldn't answer me. I yelled, "Mama! Mama!"

She didn't answer me. Mama was asleep. They were in the same room, but not in the same bed. I yelled, "Y'all get up, get up. Daddy's sick! Daddy's sick!"

We tried to get a doctor. He had gone into a coma. He had had a second stroke. We walked all night trying to get doctors. We did have a doctor who would have come, but he was out fox hunting. We called Spartanburg trying to get an ambulance, but nobody responded. He died that night. We buried him the 23rd of December 1945.

CHAPTER 3

DOMESTIC WORK

My mother was forced to look for domestic work, despite what she knew about its many limitations. For instance, domestic workers did not receive Social Security. In fact, Southern legislators had made the exclusion of their black cooks, maids, and childcare workers from Social Security, enacted in 1935, incumbent upon their votes for the bill.

According to Blanche Wiesen Cook, writing in Eleanor Roosevelt: Volume 2, The Defining Years, 1933– 1938, *"Social Security was virtually segregated racially, and women were discriminated against. Agricultural and domestic workers . . . 'casual labor' or transient, part-time, seasonal, and service workers (such as laundry and restaurant workers) . . . and local, state, and federal government employees, including teachers, were excluded from the only 'entitlements,' old-age and unemployment insurance. As a result, 80 percent of black women were excluded; 60 percent of black men were excluded, and 60 percent of white women were excluded. Only half the workforce was included"* *(281-82).*

After my father died, I said, "I have to get out of here." I always bought the *New York Times.* I saw an ad in there. Someone named Dr. Lawrence wanted somebody from the South to come to New York, and then from there to go to Martha's Vineyard to take care of children. He listed his parents' number so they could interview the person.

Mrs. Lawrence came out to Mrs. Stetson's, where I was working, and talked to me. Mrs. Stetson told her I was quite capable of taking care of children and taking care of a family.

Mrs. Lawrence bought me a ticket to New York. Vera came to see me off. We left there on the number 11 local train. I left on the 11 p.m. train and got to New York around 3 p.m. the next day; we had to change trains in Washington.

Mrs. Lawrence had told me that her son, Dr. Lawrence, worked for the Scott Paper Company, and that he would have on a gray suit. Every white man in

Pennsylvania Station had on a gray suit, so I couldn't find him.

I had his telephone number, so I called the office. One of the schoolkids who hung around the station in those days showed me how to use the payphone. I'd never used one before. The secretary told me that he was at the station looking for me. He was also calling back every five minutes to see if I had called. I told her to tell him that I was going to get a taxi and for him to go back to the office. It was on Lexington Avenue and 23rd Street.

That same kid who showed me how to use the phone helped me get a taxi. I went on to his office and his secretary was downstairs, so she could pay the taxi. I told her I had the money, but she paid.

Dr. Lawrence's secretary and I went over to Macy's to get the three uniforms I needed. That's why I don't go to Macy's now. That store was just too big. It would swallow you up.

We had to get to Woods Hole, then on to Edgartown, Massachusetts. We must have taken a six o'clock train out of Grand Central Station, going to Edgartown. Dr. Lawrence had a parlor car seat reserved for us. He didn't stay there much. I guess he went up to the lounge.

The porter came back and talked a lot to me. In fact, we exchanged addresses. He called me several times after

I got back to New York, but he was somebody I just wasn't particular about . . .

Dr. Lawrence was a warm person. He was a nice person to work for, but I really didn't get along with his spouse. Mrs. Lawrence was French. She had no feeling for anybody but herself. She didn't feel anything for the children or for her mother either. I took care of the children and did the cooking.

I met a couple and stayed friends with them for quite some time. They were related to Hulan Jack, the first black borough president.

We had a lot of fun because we had what they called an Open Door Club for all the domestic workers. Mr. Eastman, of Eastman Kodak, donated the land and built the house for the domestic workers, because there was no place there for us to go for entertainment. Whenever you were in the neighborhood, you could always go by there. All the people working there were people from outside of Massachusetts.

There was a piano there *and* a refrigerator with food in it. It was like a home away from home. You were welcome to whatever you wanted. Oaks Bluff might have had some kind of club, because it was beginning to get black people—doctors and such going to Oaks Bluff. But Edgartown was exclusive, very exclusive.

Only the wealthy, wealthy, wealthy went there. That's why it's always puzzled me about Senator Ted Kennedy saying he swam from Chappaquiddick. To get to Chappaquiddick from Edgartown you had to take the boat. And talking about that bridge . . . That was going over to another little island. There wasn't a bridge coming back to Edgartown.

Once a year we gave a high tea with cookies and sandwiches for all the wives of our employers. They were all very appreciative. People would perform—some could sing, some could dance, and some could recite.

I recited James Weldon Johnson's *Creation*. When I finished, one of the wives, who lived somewhere on Fifth Avenue and had year-old twins, asked me if I'd gone to college. I told her I wanted to go, but had to work to help support my mother and my baby sister. My father was dead, so I could not afford to go to college.

She offered to send me if I would stay there with the children when she needed me. She would have other help. I wouldn't have to stay there all the time. I don't know if it was a good offer that I let go by . . . But she said a person of my caliber should be able to go to college, and she would see that I got there. But I thought there were too many strings attached. I thought maybe if I got an education, she would want me to stay on with her. So I didn't accept it.

I can't say I regretted it, because I didn't have a chance to explore it. She called me several times after I got back to New York City, but I just didn't accept it. I never had that much patience and didn't want to confine myself to just children. I had an outlet because I could cook.

I worked for this couple in Martha's Vineyard a little over a year. Their child—Pierre—must have been about six years old; he had just started going to school. He went to a private school. There weren't any black folks around. There weren't any black folks in the park except for the domestic workers. I couldn't understand where he got the word "nigger" from. It still puzzles me. I'd never been called a nigger until I went to Martha's Vineyard. Somebody in passing might have said "there go some"—but not to my face.

I didn't say anything to the family about it, because I didn't know how much the mother or father accepted anything. So I just decided then and there that this was not the job for me. I would not stay where anybody's child called me "nigger."

That summer was a great summer. We worked, and we had a lot of fun. On Thursday just about everybody was off. We'd usually pack our lunches and plan a picnic or we'd go to Oak Bluffs. Most of the chauffeurs had use of the car on their days off, so that's how we got around.

Anyway, I decided I just wasn't going to stay. I wrote to a box number on a blind ad; it didn't have the name on it. It turned out to be Mr. Henning. He asked me to come in for an interview. They lived at 410 E.57th Street; the son was getting married. The daughter and the stepmother lived there with Mr. Henning.

I ran into some wonderful men to work for, but I didn't have that much luck with the wives. Mr. Henning called Mrs. Stetson in Greenville and she gave me a good reference. I went to work for the Hennings and I made more money, too. And there were no small children there.

I stayed there about two years. Mrs. Henning wanted me to put on white gloves to serve the food. She didn't want my hands to be seen on the tray. In fact, I had a napkin between my hands and the tray because it was hot. I asked her, "What am I going to put on my face? The hands belong to the face."

The coffee was never hot enough for her. So I boiled the cup and put the coffee in it. When she burned her lip, she didn't say anything else to me about it. The women never gave you any compliments.

I was paid in cash, $75 every two weeks. Mr. Henning paid me himself. On the first of the month, I always asked him to give me a check for $37.50 for the mortgage. This was so I didn't have to buy a money order.

He asked me, "I know it's none of my business, Jo. But what are you doing with this money?"

He was a lawyer at Goldman Sachs, so I thought he wanted to make suggestions for investment if I were sending it to a bank account. "I'm paying the mortgage on a house for my sister and my mother."

"Whose name is the property in, Jo?"

"My mother's name."

"If anything happens to her, the property will be divided among you and all your sisters and brothers, but that's your money in that house and it should come to you."

Mr. Henning went down to South Carolina and met my mother and the other sisters who were there. I had put it in my mother's name so she could feel as if she owned something. He told me I should protect myself.

That upset my mother and the other sisters and brothers, too. It didn't really matter to me, because nobody ever did anything to help me. I had the property put in my name.

Then the Hennings got a dog. I told Mrs. Henning I was not going to walk the dog. She was going to keep the dog, so I left them. But I stayed friends with Mr. Henning.

Later, Mrs. Henning came back from Europe. They had gotten rid of the dog, so I went back. I stayed there a little while until they went back to Europe. I wasn't going to be without a job, and that's when I ended up with Mrs. Cahan.

This was just before Thanksgiving in 1948. Mrs. Cahan had put an ad in the paper. She wanted a young woman to sleep in. I was trying to get away from sleeping in, but this was the only job available. I really didn't want not to be working near Christmastime. So I answered the ad and went by for an interview. The place looked strange because a lot of things were being packed up. She told me the kids' things had not been put away from camp. I accepted the job.

Wendy Cahan (the daughter) had a birthday that month. We had a beautiful party for her. The elevator guys kept looking at me strangely. Finally, about a week before they were going away, she told me that they were going to Arizona for the winter and she wouldn't need anybody.

They stayed a little later than they expected because Mr. Cahan's mother died. So I was able to work two extra weeks. I made them a big lunch, and they all got on the train to Arizona. So there I was without a job again.

I made it through the holidays even though I didn't have as much money as I wanted. Everybody who had a job at Christmastime was going to keep it. I didn't know it then, but I could have found daywork.

These cousins of mine, Ravena and Dorothy, didn't know anything either. I've never seen anybody who had been in New York as long as they had been and still didn't know anything about finding work. I rented a room in Dorothy's apartment.

Domestic workers didn't have unemployment then because we didn't pay into Social Security; we didn't have any benefits. That bothered me a long time about the domestic workers. I was very grateful when we did get Social Security in 1951, because we worked hard. Sometimes you ran into somebody who would pay you—but the average employer didn't pay you when you were out sick.

I went looking to get jobs in restaurants, but every place I went to seemed to look at me and say I wasn't the type for restaurant work. When I didn't get a job, my father tried to help me in a dream.

I never knew anything about playing numbers. But I did know that Pa had said when he told me to take care of my mother and my sister, that he didn't have any money to leave, but there would always be a way made for me.

I didn't have but twenty dollars. So I was going to go downtown to look for a job on Monday.

And lo and behold, Sunday night I dreamed about Pa. He came into the window and had on a pair of overalls like those he worked in when he was on the farm.

"Now you need my help. Put all you got on 281."

"Daddy, you never gambled in your life. Why tell me to gamble?"

"Well, this is the only way I can help you."

I knew what he was talking about from Cousin Ravena, who played the numbers; she dreamed them and she played them. But I just wasn't getting involved.

I went downtown again looking for a job. I thought that maybe I could become a maid in the hotels. I was five feet five. And I guess I weighed 102 pounds soaking wet. I think it was more my size than anything else. They felt like the work was too heavy for me.

But I could basically lift what some people who weigh 150 or 200 pounds couldn't, because I had followed my father around. And I understood how it's a certain way that you position yourself so that you could move things.

I went back uptown and stopped by Cousin Ravena's house. She and her husband, Clarence, had a restaurant at 120th Street. It was her sister, Dorothy, who also did domestic work, that I was living with.

Ravena was just so into numbers that she told Clarence, "Go out and find out what the first number is." He came back and said two numbers were out: 2 and 8.

I shook my head.

Ravena said, "What you shaking your head for, Jo?"

"I got ten dollars. Here, Clarence, take it and put it on the 'one.' That number is going to be 281."

She said, "How you know?"

"Dad came into the room last night and told me to play it, but I went downtown to look for a job and I didn't play it. Just put this ten dollars on the one."

That was the single action. I didn't know what it was called then. So . . . it did come out. It was straight: 281.

Not being a believer in playing the numbers, it didn't bother me. It was 8:1 then, so I got eighty dollars. I gave Clarence five dollars for putting it in for me. So I had seventy-five dollars. That was about two weeks' salary. I had enough to help me look for another job.

Then I went to work for two lawyers who lived on 91st Street and Central Park West, the Bakers. It seems that most of the time I worked in families with lawyers. I think I stayed there from January until Mrs. Cahan came back from Arizona. She must have come back around the last of May and the first of June, after school was out down in Arizona.

She hurriedly put this call through, asking me would I come back. She knew she was wrong, and she was sorry. But they had already made this plan. She liked me, but she didn't want to tell me, because she knew I wouldn't take the job. She gave me a week's salary to leave the Bakers and come back to her. I wasn't satisfied where I was working, so I said to myself, "What do I have to lose?"

I was kind of tired of living with Dorothy, too. She had had a lot of emotional problems with her son and her daughter-in-law.

I still don't know today how I survived. Most of the time I was there I didn't get an hour's sleep. She would talk half the night. Then after she stopped talking, I couldn't go to sleep. And I had to get up and go to work.

She wanted her son to marry this young woman at first, and then she didn't want him to marry her. He married her anyway. Then here came the grandchild.

I guess Dorothy still wanted to be first in his life. But now he had a wife and a child, so they should have been first. They were living with her, so finally she threw them out.

That was when all the burden fell on me, for her to talk, talk, talk half of the night. I went to the doctor and asked him if he would give her some sleeping pills so she could go to sleep. Dr. Wilson was a friend of the family. He did give her something to rest her nerves, but she still talked. I was glad to go so I could get some sleep. I think if I had stayed there another month or so, I might have had a nervous breakdown.

I was off Thursday and Sunday. But I went in and made breakfast on Thursday, so I couldn't sleep then. Of course, you couldn't sleep if you stayed in the house with Dorothy anyway. So I decided for health reasons it was best to go back to Mrs. Cahan. The Cahans didn't go to the country that summer.

The next year, 1950, we went up to Pound Ridge and rented a house. We got along all right. I must have worked there about a year or so. But finally, I decided I didn't want to sleep in anymore. I could see myself not getting anywhere, and I was getting older.

I think Mrs. Baker and Mrs. Cahan are the only people I ever left where I just left the key inside the mailbox. I'd had enough of them.

Mrs. Cahan and I had had some misunderstandings. She couldn't understand why I was tired of staying in at night. I felt like when we got Social Security in 1951, they should have given us some work hours. We shouldn't have had to work around the clock.

I'd gotten sick. The children had a cold, and I got the flu. This was the last of March. She wasn't going to pay me, for a whole week. It was one of the few times I had the flu. I can remember having it three times in my life. The flu, not a cold.

I sat down and said to her, "Mrs. Cahan, I got sick from waiting on your children. That's how I caught the flu. I took care of them and I got them well. And you mean to tell me that you're not going to pay me? How could you be so cruel? My rent went on. I had to eat. I had to pay the doctor. I didn't go to the doctor; he came to the house (it was Doctor Wilson) and gave me an injection. If Mr. Cahan's secretary gets sick, I know he has some way to take care of her while she is out sick. Now, if you want me, somebody's going to have to pay me. This is not fair."

"I did the work."

"Nobody did the work. I had to do it. You bought some food, but nobody did the cleaning. The woman came in and cleaned, but nobody did the light dusting."

"All right, Jo. I'll pay you. All right."

She was paying me $50 a week then. Whenever I left her and came back to her, she had to give me some more money.

But I was tired of sleeping in. Even though Thursday was my day off, she always made sure she had company on Wednesday night, so I couldn't come home. If I had come home, it would have been 3 o'clock in the morning. I had to wash the dishes and everything before I left.

So I stayed until Thursday morning. I'd get the children up for her, let her sleep, and send them off to school. Then I would leave. Sometimes I stayed to give Mrs. Cahan breakfast. Sometimes I would leave as soon as I got the kids off to school. They usually had to leave around 7:30. I was also off on Sunday mornings, but I had to stay there Saturday night.

Mr. Cahan wasn't demanding. He was great. He understood people who had to work. But Mrs. Cahan didn't.

One morning I was late getting back Friday morning and Mrs. Cahan told me that I had to be there on time.

"Look, Mrs. Cahan, you know I stay and take care of the children sometimes on a Thursday morning, so what's wrong with you getting up this morning and giving them breakfast? I need a job and you need somebody to work for you, so I'm not going to tolerate this. I told you I was sorry, but I just didn't wake up, that's all. You know what time it was when I went to bed Wednesday night, which was early Thursday morning.

And I got up early Thursday morning and gave the kids breakfast. I'm not going to tolerate you saying anything to me about it. I can leave right now."

"Oh, no. Oh, no, Jo."

"All right, just don't—I can't take any more of it. Those are your children."

I had already gotten her straightened out about cooking the eggs.

I sat her down one morning and said, "Mrs. Cahan, if somebody can't do things to suit you, the best thing is to do it yourself. I tried cooking this egg every way that I can, and it never suits you.

"I'm going to leave the egg and the margarine out here. I've already made the coffee. I'll have the piece of bread sitting beside the toaster. From now on out, you get your own breakfast, hear, because I can't take any more of it."

I made four different breakfasts, five if I ate mine. Everybody ate at different times and ate different stuff. Robert had to have his first, Wendy had hers second, and then Mr. Cahan. If I ate any, that was number four, and hers was the last. Sometimes Robert wanted lamb chops. For breakfast!

A friend of the family, Mrs. Brown, was doing work for an agency called Taylor Maid Service. You didn't have to sleep in. You did work and you were paid by the hour. You did have some benefits—New York State Disability—but they didn't take out unemployment insurance. I went down for an interview one Thursday when I was off and filled out the application.

"With a recommendation from Mrs. Brown, I know you must be great. I don't have to wait for the bonding to come back. You can start Monday."

I worked for Mrs. Cahan that Friday and Saturday. Sunday morning she was always in bed. I got the kids off to Sunday school. It was Hebrew school, but they called it Sunday school.

I just left the key beside the toaster on Sunday morning when I left. She didn't call me all day Sunday. I guess she thought I forgot the key. When she called Monday morning, I was gone.

My cousin Dorothy's grandson answered the phone. When Mrs. Cahan called, he told her I had gone to another job; he sat around and listened to all the conversations. I think he was about five years old, but he was grown from the day he was born. I didn't call her back, so she finally called me that night.

"When you got ready to go to Arizona, you left me. I could not work out a two-week notice, because I had this job already and I didn't have time to wait."

"All right, All right!" she screamed.

Taylor Maid Service, the company I was working for at the time, wasn't paying into Social Security, but this was '51, so I had my Social Security number. You had to be bonded and fingerprinted. I passed all that. We had apartments which we cleaned, maybe four or five a day. Usually he'd group us in neighborhoods so you wouldn't have to lose so much in traveling time. Or all your jobs would be in one building. They were just beginning to build these very large apartment buildings for the wealthy people.

The one that I worked in most was at No. 1 Fifth Avenue. This is where I did meet a lot of nice people. They'd leave you a sandwich for your lunch and they would leave you a tip. And if they didn't leave you food for lunch, some of them would leave you money and tell you to get your lunch. Most of the guys liked to cook, and they'd fix you whatever they had for their dinner that night and leave it in the refrigerator. You never found food or money for lunch in the ladies' apartments. And very rarely did they leave you a tip.

We just cleaned. You made the bed and did some light vacuuming. You took care of their bedroom just the same as maid service in a hotel. Sometimes the guys would leave a couple of pairs of socks for you to wash for them. But you didn't do any other laundry. The ladies would want you to do their laundry. These were bachelorettes, single women. Sometimes you'd find a family.

After I left, Mrs. Cahan hired a lady, but she couldn't make the dinner parties. It's hard to find a person who worked in service who could do what I could do with food. I think Mr. Cahan kept on after her to ask me to come back.

Finally, she called and asked would I come to cook and serve her dinner parties. So I told her yeah, I'd come. She'd pay me more, that's all.

If I had a party for Mrs. Cahan, I wouldn't do one for Taylor Maid Service. I did more of the parties than I did the maid work—the cleaning. Once I was established with the Taylor Maid clients, word of mouth went from one to the other that I was a good cook and I was a great waitress.

I thought it didn't mean anything, but the owner had all these notes on the wall from people I did parties for, telling him how great my service was.

I had a group that if they couldn't get me, they didn't have their dinner party that night. I always got good tips.

They paid Taylor Maid a certain amount, and he gave us a percentage. We were paid more for cooking than we were for cleaning, so I made good money. It was minimum wage with a little more for cooking.

Then I found a lady who wanted somebody every evening. I decided I wasn't going to work for Taylor Maid anymore in the evening. I would clean, but I stopped cooking for Taylor Maid unless it was somebody who just wanted lunch.

Every evening from four until after dinner, I worked for Mrs. Leonard at 72nd Street and Third Avenue, and she was nice people, too. Taylor Maid would send her somebody every evening, but she wouldn't get the same person. Going there on my own, I could make more money because there was no agency cut coming out of it. She paid me five dollars every evening, five evenings a week.

CHAPTER 4

LIFE WITH LEN

The internationally-known Savoy—in existence from 1926 to 1958—was a two-story ballroom spanning the block from 140th to 141st Street on Lenox Avenue in Harlem. A black-and-white marquee beckoned passersby in to dance. Nicknamed by the actress Lana Turner "the Home of Happy Feet," the Savoy's 250- by 50-foot wooden floor could hold up to 4,000 dancers at a time, which is undoubtedly why it had to be replaced every three years. "Stompin' at the Savoy," the instrumental composed by Edgar Sampson and Chick Webb in 1934, reflected the joy of dancing there.

The Savoy had a much freer atmosphere than Roseland, the popular downtown ballroom. At Roseland, blacks and whites were restricted to one weekly night of dancing divided by a rope down the middle of the room, while the Savoy welcomed people of all races dancing together. This is one of the legendary places where Mama enjoyed her hard-won free time and where she met my father.

I was able to go dancing at the Savoy. I had extra money and I had time. I didn't have to worry about getting home to get up to go to work. Usually I went to the Savoy on Thursday and Friday nights. It had a bandstand and a dance floor. There were tables around it and there were seats around the wall where you could sit, too. The entranceway was downstairs on the first floor, where you paid. There were dim lights around, kind of romantic. The bright lights were over the bandstand. It was not a fancy place.

They had whiskey, and you could bring something to eat, but they didn't sell food. It was strictly dancing. The jitterbug, the slow drag, whatever you could do, they had the music for you to do it to. Most of the time there were two bands: the house band and the visiting band.

Single women hardly went on Saturday night because most of them were at work, since most of them slept in. When you slept in, the employers didn't eat dinner until seven. Then you had to do the dishes and serve them all.

That Friday night I had had a dinner party. But I liked that better than I did sleeping in, because whenever I got finished, I left. My time was my own. I only went sometimes on Saturday night. I did go on a Saturday night when I met Len.

Me and my older sister, Vera, went to the Savoy. Vera was here in New York by then. Sally, my younger sister, had been here and gone back. This was Len's 30th birthday: June 14, 1952. He was a great dancer. I couldn't dance that well. But he seemed to enjoy me anyway. I had on a flowery dress with a white background.

Our eyes caught, then he asked me to dance. Len was about five feet seven and a half inches tall, a little bit taller than I was. He was wearing a gray suit, a white shirt, and a grayish-blue tie. He never wore a hat in the summer. He didn't want his hair to get messed up. We didn't wear sports clothes; you had to be dressed up to go to the Savoy.

His cousins were there, too. The house band and whoever stayed at the Savoy were there. Buddy Johnson was the guest artist that night. The singer was his sister, Ella Johnson, and she was singing *Since I Fell for You.* That was the song we were dancing to when I met Len.

There was always a crowd. We must have gotten there around ten-thirty or eleven o'clock and stayed until around one o'clock. Len took the Lenox Avenue bus with me down to 116th Street. Then we got off the bus and walked over to Seventh Avenue and Dewey Square Park. We sat in that park and talked awhile.

The first night I saw him, he asked me did I want to get married. I told him no. He told me about being in the Navy, having five sisters and three brothers, and that he was from Richmond, Virginia. We talked a lot. Then he got my telephone number. He lived at 115th Street over near Manhattan Avenue.

That next evening we went out. One of the things that attracted me to him was that he and I both liked to go to the park. Then we went up to Mount Morris Park and went over to the bell tower. I'd been going up there long before I got married. So we went up there and we stayed awhile.

Then I came back by Cousin Ravena's and got something to eat. He said he wanted to go to the show, but he liked the shoot-'em-ups and I didn't want to go see that, so we didn't go to the movie. We went back down to Dewey Square Park again. We sat down and talked a long time.

I didn't see him that week at night, because I was working every evening, but I saw him Saturday. We went somewhere down around Mulberry Street. There were a lot of dance places around then, mostly Latin dance places. But Len could dance to anything.

Over the next few weeks, we'd either go to the movies, or we'd go back to the Savoy or to the Apollo Theater if somebody was there who wasn't at the Savoy that we wanted to see. We both liked music.

He met Vera that first night, and in the next couple of days or weeks he met Bill, who later became my sister's husband, so sometimes we would all go to the movies together.

We were going backwards and forwards and back and forth. Then I decided I was going to get married. We went to get the blood test. You had to wait thirty days then until you could get the license.

That was when the mix-up in the dates came in. There was always somebody standing down there saying: "We're preachers. We'll marry you." I said to him, "Let's go to a real church where we know the preacher is ordained." This was August in 1952 when we started getting these things together, because we were going to get married in September.

No, he decided that a guy who handed you a card that said he's a preacher was going to marry us. So we got married in a little storefront over on Manhattan Avenue and 116th Street, right near where he was living.

It was early November when we found out that he was not ordained. So then on November the 6th, we had to get a real preacher. We had our reception on December the 6th. By this time I was pregnant.

Here came the fun, trying to get him to get an apartment. He wanted to stay in that hole that he was in. But he lived in a single room; it was too small! I was still living with Cousin Dorothy. I didn't want to live with her, and I didn't want to stay in his room. You couldn't find an apartment then; nobody wanted to rent to someone with a baby. But we stayed in his room until it was almost time for the baby to be born.

Dorothy told me she'd contacted this lady at 112th Street, so we moved. We had a room at 120 W. 112th Street I bought myself a mattress, Dorothy gave us a bed, and I bought the table and chairs, which I still have. By this time, Mr. Henning was dead and I got a lot of pots and pans from Mrs. Henning, the lady I used to work for.

Dorothy's friend had lived in this apartment since the 1940s. She had been lucky enough to get money to buy a home up in the Bronx. Instead of turning this apartment back to the landlord so he could rent it to another family, she used it to subsidize herself, which meant to rent rooms. Every room in it—like the dining room—became a bedroom for a couple and a child. The second front room that later became our living room was a bedroom. This was our room: mine, Len's, and soon to be the baby's, too.

Where we lived was actually an apartment building with apartments for 24 families, six floors with four apartments on each floor. There might've been two apartments on each floor in earlier years. The apartment was supposed to be for a family of four. They had been homes for the wealthy people. Mostly doctors lived in our building when Harlem was a Jewish and Italian neighborhood.

Another couple lived in the large room in the back. And a guy lived in the small single room further back there. Everybody shared the kitchen and the bath. Most of the time there were eight people in the house, but sometimes it became ten. She charged you per room. Our room was $25 per week.

In the meantime, I'd stopped working for Taylor Maid about six months before. It was too much going from place to place. I went back to Mrs. Cahan. I didn't go every evening, because her son, Robert, was away in boarding school. Wendy Cahan was trying to find out when the baby was coming.

I don't know how much Mrs. Cahan had told Wendy about my pregnancy. She was only eight years old.

She said to me, "Jo, you're getting fat, but you're getting fat in one place. I thought when you got fat, you got fat all over."

"That's why I didn't want to get fat. I told you to stop feeding me." When she'd go out and get candy, she would always get me something.

Her aunt, Mrs. Cahan's sister, said to me, "Jo, how are you feeling?"

"I'm feeling fine."

"Is it moving yet?"

"Yes."

Wendy looked up at me and stormed, "You're making a baby and nobody told me. That's what you're doing!"

Her aunt took her aside and told her yes, that I was pregnant.

Then Wendy came back into the kitchen and said, "If the baby is a girl, it's got to be named Wendy, because we don't name any Wendys after us." (Ashkenazic Jewish custom forbids naming newborns after living relatives.)

"Wendy, that's your name. You have to consult your mother about that. If it's a girl, I don't care what it's named, but if it's a boy, it's named for the father."

"It's gonna be a girl, it's gonna be a girl. It'll be named Wendy."

Here came Robert. He had a little friend named Diane. He wanted the baby named Diane.

"No, Robert. If it's a girl, Wendy can name it. If it's a boy, it's named for the father."

Then he pulled on Wendy's hair, because he didn't intend for her to win any battles. But she had won this battle.

When Mrs. Cahan came in, Wendy told her the whole story.

"Did you ask Jo?"

"Jo said it was all right. And I want a Wendy. That's what I want; I want a Wendy."

Wendy fed me and Robert fed me and everybody fed me. Everybody looked after me after they found out what was going on. If something dropped, someone would pick it up. When Robert went to the store, he wanted to know what I wanted. One day I told him to bring me some watermelon.

I wasn't going to let anything upset me. I was going to develop this child without any headaches or any problems. After the child got here, then we'd see about taking care of the child. But I was going to develop a healthy child. That's all that I was concerned about. Somebody talking about hair and all that, that didn't matter; I just asked God to give me a healthy child.

I had an easy pregnancy. Everybody talked about morning sickness . . . I felt woozy a couple of times, but I never did become nauseated like a lot of other people did. I knew it was something that was there for nine months, then it had to come out, because it couldn't come up! There weren't all these pains and all this sitting down. I just kept on working.

One day in May, Mrs. Cahan was sick and wanted me to make her some chicken soup—I went down there to make that chicken soup.

When I was getting in the taxi that evening going to Mrs. Cahan's, the taxicab driver looked back at me and said: "Miss, there's no hospital down there."

"No, I know there isn't. One day this week, but not today." "All right, then. You be careful." Yellow cabs came up to Harlem then.

I told Mrs. Cahan: "Now look, I'm not coming down here anymore. It's time for this baby to be born, and I don't want it born in no taxi."

"I'll take you to the hospital from down here, Jo."

"I don't want you to take me to no hospital. I'm not coming back down here until after the baby's born."

When I was going back to Harlem, the driver asked me where I was going and if I was all right. I told him I was going home and I was all right. That particular cabdriver got out and opened the door for me. Then he saw me up the steps of the front stoop.

Len looked for work. He'd do some daywork in construction. Or he'd drive a truck. Usually he'd get a job with a demolition crew. I still have the silver baby rattle that he found in one of the buildings that he was doing demolition on. It has "Jr." engraved on it.

As soon as I could go back to work full-time, I was going back to work. I thought maybe Len would find steady work . . . but he didn't. I had a little money, so it just didn't bother me. I paid the rent.

The day after I came back home from Mrs. Cahan's, I cleaned up the refrigerator and bought the bottles. I wanted it nice and clean when I came home from the hospital so I would have somewhere to keep the baby's milk. A friend gave me some diapers.

Everybody helped me get ready for the baby. A friend bought the baby the things to come home in, the layette. I had made a little dress, in case it was a girl. I didn't see the sense in buying a lot of things. And Dorothy got some baby bibs.

The pregnancy went well. I went in the hospital at 7 o'clock in the morning, five days after I had worked for Mrs. Cahan. The doctor came and checked me when we were in. He said the baby was due around 12:30 or 1 o'clock. He was going up to Mother Cabrini Hospital, which was on Edgecombe Avenue then, to look in on another patient. The doctor said he would be back, but he didn't get back in time for the baby to be born.

The nurse came to check on me—I was in one of the holding rooms—and she started screaming: "Oh, the baby's coming! The baby's coming! Get her together!" They got me up to the delivery room, but the baby was almost there when we got there.

Sure enough, here came a girl. Her name was Wendy, Wendy Dianna Jones. Since Mama was named Anna, I just made it Dianna instead of Wendy Anna. I kept sounding it out.

When the doctor did come, I hadn't seen the baby. He said to me: "Mrs. Jones, you've just had a baby girl"—he said he delivered her, but I know he wasn't there—"and she has more instinct than any baby I've ever delivered; you take care of her."

When I saw her, she was holding one finger up. That's why I knew Wendy must have been able to see. Most babies have their hands curled up, but Wendy was holding her index finger on her left hand up straight like she was looking at it. I mashed it down, to see if there was anything wrong, and I looked at all her toes.

Wendy was always moving and alert, and her eyes were bright. She had a bright smile on her face. There must have been something about the expression on her face that made the doctor feel that she was different. I went back to him afterwards and he recommended a pediatrician.

When Wendy graduated from high school, I sent Dr. Meriden a letter and clippings of her winning the National Merit Scholarship. He wrote a nice letter back. He was as proud of her as I was. Our little girl, he called her, and he said to keep him posted.

After I gave birth, all of a sudden, Len was going to name the baby. He'd been defeated: It was a girl. But he was going to name the baby anyway. His niece sent a list, about fifteen or twenty names. She hadn't written; she hadn't said anything until then. He picked out Princess.

Since we couldn't agree on a name, we just put "girl" on the birth certificate.

It was my decision now. I didn't know his niece from anybody. Dorothy and Mrs. Troutman, the landlady, said, well, maybe that's what caused him not to do anything. But he wasn't doing anything in the beginning, so I didn't see that as being part of his not getting up and going to work; the name wasn't the problem.

Mrs. Cahan had been to the hospital and she had brought a dozen roses and sent a telegram. By the time we came home, she had got the carriage and sent a white wicker bassinet that had belonged to Robert and her Wendy. Len and I had an old car then. She bought a stroller you could take out and strap into the car.

The Cahans went to the house they had in Pound Ridge, New York, after my Wendy was born.

I didn't go. That's the year I worked in the book factory for two weeks. I had found the job just before Len and I had a fight. I made $35 a week. I had never seen human beings work in such hazardous conditions and such filth in all my life. I was just going to stay there until Mrs. Cahan came back from the country.

And then here I had trouble with Len. I still don't know what happened to him. I couldn't understand why he didn't want to work.

The fight started because he wanted the rent money. He said he wanted to play cards. If he lost the money, what would I have to pay rent with when the landlady came?

We had to pay $25 a week for that room. He hadn't worked that week. I had worked and I had the rent money. It was a Saturday evening. Because I didn't want to give him the money, he jumped on me. There were people in the house, but they didn't want to intervene.

Finally, I got him off me. I woke Wendy up and left her with another roomer in the house, Red Lucy. I went to the police station, the 28th Precinct. The precinct was located where the Ennis Francis Houses are now on 123rd Street. They called the policeman on the beat and he came over. He was white.

The policeman told Len to leave. He said: "What's wrong? You can find a job. Get a job and take care of your family. Come on and go with me. Don't come back here tonight. Don't do your wife like this." So Len left.

Sunday morning Len wanted to come back down there annoying me, so I called the police again. This time they came in the patrol car. If I had to call them again, they said they would have to take him to jail. Len said he came back to get some things.

The police said, "Whatever you want, we'll stand here until you get it. But you're not going in this house alone." I gave him his shirt and a pair of pants and that Nu Nile, stupid hair grease. He wasn't going nowhere without that!

So he went down to Atlantic City. He called to tell me he went down there to work the week. Len could cook, too. He was trained as a baker in the Navy. Why wouldn't he do one of these things to help so we could survive? He said he wasn't going to work for peanuts. But whatever money he made, we could have used it.

I wasn't going on that job with my face swollen up. So I didn't go back to the book factory. I went there the next week and got my money, but I didn't go back to work.

In the meantime, Vera was pregnant and was ready to deliver. She went to the hospital and Nina and Nelson were born in August of 1953. She was already in the hospital when me and Len got to fighting that first time. I didn't go down there that Sunday because my lips were swollen; one of the roomers, Red Lucy, went. I don't know whether Red Lucy told Vera about the fight or not.

I didn't go to work Friday—that's why I didn't have any money—because I had to take Vera to the hospital Thursday. She'd been keeping Wendy. So now there wasn't anybody to keep her.

Len stayed down in Atlantic City about two weeks. Black Lucy (there were two Lucys rooming in the apartment) was begging me to go to the relief, go to the relief.

"I can't go to the relief."

"You have to tell them you don't know who the father is."

"I know there ain't no need for me to go. I'm definitely going to say who the father is. I'll tell them I don't know where he is, but I'm never gonna say I don't know who the father is."

I hadn't grown up seeing anything like this. Big Ma and Big Pa didn't argue. My mother would start asking him questions. Rather than discuss anything in front of us, he just took a walk. Then he'd come back. I don't know what they did at night after they got in the bed, whether they discussed it again or not. But they didn't resume their argument in front of us.

I wasn't going to accept getting beat up from anyone. My second oldest sister had gone through that, but I knew I couldn't accept it.

When Len came back from Atlantic City, he didn't have any money or a job. He started doing daywork again. But he'd work maybe one or two days out of the week and lie down the rest. He would stay in bed drinking water and reading detective stories.

I never understood why he didn't work. There were just so many things that he *could* have done but he just would not *apply* himself to any job—not long at a time.

Everywhere he went, they liked him. Len had a job at New York Telephone. He was one of the construction foremen who would take care of the buildings and maintain the telephone lines. New York Telephone had different buildings throughout New York City and throughout New York State, too.

The telephone company boss gave him a company car so he could travel around. He even kept it on the weekends. They finally pulled the car off the street.

They would call to tell him to come to work, and he said he was going. Then he would leave the house and wouldn't go.

He was in the Navy four years. I wonder if when the men came out of the service, they had been under such discipline maybe they didn't want to be on a structured job anymore.

He got work with the post office. They hired substitutes during the Christmas rush. The last time he got a substitute job with the post office, he brought his bag, jacket, and cap to the house and left them there. Finally one of the inspectors came out to get them.

Shortly after we got married, he wanted to live in the projects. I didn't want to live there because there were too many folks there. But I wanted to move because I knew we were paying too much rent.

I wanted to get these two houses. They were on 84th Street and Columbus Avenue. That area had gone down, just like Harlem. The city let all poor areas go down, then they'd have to spend hundreds and hundreds of dollars to redevelop them. They were SROs, single-room occupancy buildings, but they hadn't cut the rooms up like they had in Harlem.

I had seen an article in the *New York Times* about these programs. People wouldn't pay their taxes, so the houses reverted to the city. There were two houses with one boiler. I went down to see about it. I think they were ten thousand dollars apiece.

Len wouldn't go. He was a GI; he could have gotten help from the GI Bill. He could have taken care of the baby and taken care of the houses. I would work on a regular job. He could fix up the houses. And what he couldn't do, we could pay somebody else to do.

We could live in one apartment and rent out the others; then we would have enough to pay the mortgage. He wouldn't have to worry about going to work because he would have a job. We could have had a good life.

But he said, "You South Carolina women always want something." He said that he didn't want no house; he didn't need no house. That was when I decided that there wasn't any hope for our relationship—our marriage— lasting. I would never be able to accomplish the things that I wanted to do with Wendy if I had a negative partner. After that, he started beating and knocking on me, and I was through.

I continued to pay rent and buy food for all of us. But I knew that couldn't last. I wasn't making but $45 a week, and that was not enough to pay $25 a week for rent and buy food for us. So I was in the process of looking for a second job.

But I didn't understand why I should have to look for a second job to take care of all of us with him still there. I didn't mind looking for a second job if there was just myself and Wendy to take care of. All through September, he didn't bother to get a job.

That September was when I got the permanent job at Standard Brands. Vera and Red Lucy took care of Wendy. Then in October, my sister Sally came back. She'd been down south about two years.

One Friday evening in November I had come home from work and Len wanted to go out. He wanted to beat me up again, because he didn't have any money and wanted mine. Len told me to put the baby down in the bassinet.

"Don't put your hands on me no more!" I had a butcher knife in the bassinet. When I laid Wendy down, I was going to pick up the butcher knife and stab him in the neck.

Sally was in the kitchen, but he didn't know it. She came out with a hammer in her hand and said, "If you put your hands on her, you'll die. You'd better get out of here now!" He left without any money that evening.

Red Lucy and the other roomers didn't want Sally to come help me. They told her it was none of her business. Sally had her faults, but she had some times—in tight spots—when she came through for me.

I wasn't his child. He wasn't going to beat me. I told him I wasn't going to take it anymore. "How can you say you love me and want to beat me and scar me up?"

I could see that it was impossible to maintain the family as a whole. I would not take abuse. The only thing I knew to do was separate.

I decided I wasn't going to buy any more food for him. I had asked him to just leave us alone and said we'd be all right. I couldn't take care of all of us. It was the last of November, and the hospital bill for Wendy's birth hadn't been paid.

On November 30th, when I came home, he had gone. That was 1953. Sally was there when he left. She was crying, but I told her, "Don't cry." I could take care of Wendy and myself.

He came back on December 4th to get some blankets. I told him the blankets were mine.

He had gotten a room somewhere here in the city. Around Christmas, he came by, but I wasn't there. He left a maroon dress for Wendy with Red Lucy. He said he had some money for shoes for the baby, but he didn't give it to Red Lucy.

Wendy and I had gone down to Mrs. Cahan's so she could give Wendy her Christmas toy; I have the picture of Wendy sitting on the floor down there next to big Wendy.

I told Mr. Cahan that Len was gone. That was when Mr. Cahan told me about his first marriage ending in divorce and that it comes to all of us. Mr. Cahan told me that he would help me legally. If we needed anything else, the family was there for us. But since I was a strong woman, he thought I would be able to take care of the baby.

He did encourage me to go to family court and take out a nonsupport warrant.

"He's not working."

"It may come a time when he'll say he's supporting you and he's not, and you won't have any proof. They won't take your word against his word. You won't have any proof unless you've gone to family court and he's supposed to pay and he doesn't. We'll see if we can't get you a legal separation."

We made it through that Christmas . . . all right. It was sad. But then you know that the pain wouldn't be as bad as if we had had to live in an abusive household throughout our lives. It was painful then, but I realized that for us to survive I would have to assume the responsibility of mother and father. I gave him up. From then on, I took care of Wendy.

Mr. Cahan filled out the papers for the legal separation. They were received, but they weren't signed and sent back. When we went to court, the first time he didn't show up. The second time, he did show up, but there wasn't any money there. And the third time, his sister had given him some money, so I think it was $30 or $40 that I got. I kept going backwards and forth, and then he just stopped coming at all.

A warrant was issued, but they could never find him. They never did arrest him.

Finally, the warrant officer called me and asked me what decision had I made.

"Just drop it. The baby and I are doing all right, so just cancel the warrant."

"All right, we'll cancel it. We've been looking for him for a year, and we haven't been able to find him."

I think Wendy was about four when we met him on the street. Somehow, God just dropped him out of the blue. I looked up the street and there he was, on Lenox Avenue and 116th Street coming down Lenox.

She had just asked me if she had a father. I told her everybody had a father, but hers didn't live with us.

"Here comes your father now, baby. This is your father coming here now."

I stopped and spoke to him. I don't know whether he was embarrassed or what he was. But he told Wendy he wasn't her father, that he was her uncle. I told him to stop lying to his daughter.

"You know you're her father. Don't lie to her."

Wendy had never seen him that much to know him. So she really didn't know whether he was her father or not.

I had a friend that Wendy had been calling father. She just started calling Jim "Daddy." He didn't stop her, and neither did I. Wendy called him Daddy because he was always warm and receptive to her when she met him. He lived in the 119th Street and Seventh Avenue area. We always had to pass by there when we were going to Ravena's house, so Wendy had seen him quite often. He had also visited the house, because he was a friend that I knew before I got married.

"No, he says he's not my father."

Then we walked over to Seventh Avenue and we saw my friend. Wendy said that was her father. I said, "No, he's not your father. We just left your father." When Wendy got older, she realized Jim was not her father.

Sometime later, Len knocked on my door. I didn't open the door, but he told me he'd been in an accident. He needed the birth certificate for Wendy so he could get some support for himself and some for her. I told him I didn't think it would do any good, but I'd take the birth certificate up to the Social Security office.

I asked him was he going to help me support Wendy. He was thinking I could take Wendy and go on the relief.

"I won't have to go on the relief because I have a job. You may be on the relief, but your baby won't be there and neither will I. I'm as much of a woman as my father was a man. I can take care of this one."

When he got in this accident, he couldn't get any disability from Social Security, but the Navy had to give him disability. Wendy didn't qualify for any because my salary was so high. I wouldn't have accepted it anyway.

He had lost one of his arms; he really couldn't work then. One of his eyes was out. He said a car hit him. No one got in touch with me, so I never knew what really happened. Later I heard he stayed in a coma for about six weeks. I didn't hear any more from him for a long time.

When he was getting on disability, I did get a number of requests that I pay partial support for him. There again, Mr. Cahan came to our rescue. He got a lawyer for me. I had to send affidavits from the preacher and from the school that I was supporting Wendy.

Then—I don't know about now—there was a New York State law that if you were married, if you weren't divorced, you were responsible for part of your husband's financial support.

Each year I would get that statement. What I did was just tell them to look in the files; I wasn't making any more money, so I stopped sending in the forms.

Finally, Len got cancer of the esophagus. I guess he got it from drinking, not eating properly, and smoking. Sometimes I wonder if he was sick before. That maybe he had the beginning symptoms of cancer before and it just showed up so many years later.

So he went into the hospital. That's when his brother, Ellis, called me. Ellis asked me did I want to come see Len. I told him we hadn't been in close contact with each other, but if Len wanted me to come, I'd come.

When I went to the hospital, I saw that it was the end. I knew that his family wasn't seeing about him. It hurt. But what can you do when you don't have control? We were legally separated. Len listed Ellis as next of kin.

But in the end, Ellis tried to put me in control, so I could pay for the funeral. When I discussed it with Mr. Cahan, he said he didn't know why I should be responsible for the funeral when Len hadn't been a father to Wendy. I refused to pay for the funeral. He took Len back to Virginia for burial. Ellis was cruel. The obituary didn't mention me or Wendy. She was thirteen when Len died.

As far as I was concerned, I had no hatred. I always told Wendy that we couldn't say that he deserted us and took care of another family. He didn't take care of his self.

FAMILY

1. BIG PA

2. BIG MA

3. LEN JONES

4. EARLY DAYS AT STANDARD BRANDS

CHAPTER 5

FAMILY BURDENS

As was often the case in my mother's life, major events overlapped in time. Mama was dealing with the abuse from my father, Vera's problems, the start of her new position at Standard Brands, and the struggle to get the apartment, described in Chapter 6, simultaneously.

That Sunday night after that first fight with Len, I didn't go see Vera because I didn't want her to know that Len had hit me. This was August 1953. I bought Red Lucy some flowers for Vera and gave her carfare to go down to the hospital to see Vera.

I had to stay off from work when Vera went into the hospital because I didn't have anybody to take care of Wendy. I carried Vera to the hospital Thursday, so I hadn't gone to the book factory on Friday. They held back one week's pay, so I hadn't gotten paid.

I went to see Vera the week after the babies were born. She had to stay in the hospital a little longer because of the two births. She didn't have any prenatal care, so no one knew she was expecting twins. Even if she had been on the relief, she wouldn't have had care. They didn't give you anything until you gave birth. Nina and Nelson must've been about two weeks old when she came out of the hospital.

I was thinking everything was going on all right. Then she called me to come get her, because she was going to put the children up for adoption. I said, "What? . . . All right, I'll be down there. We have to talk."

The social worker said, "Yes, your sister said she had three children already, and she couldn't take care of these two."

"I know that. But she knew she had three children from her first marriage. Our father and mother took care of us. I will not stand by and let her send my father's and my mother's blood to some stranger. I will not do it. If a social worker will help us, she will take these children home."

I had already gotten the call to go to Standard Brands to help out for vacation. I told the social worker I was going to work and I would share the money with Vera until she got better so she could work. "She can bring her babies to my house and we can get somebody to come in and take care of all three of them. But she's not going to give the babies away."

"Vera, you ought to be ashamed of yourself. You knew you could get pregnant and that you and Bill weren't married. You have three children. Now you have two more. Why do you want to give them away?"

"I can't take care of them alone."

"You oughta thought about that before you got pregnant, Vera. There is no need you getting that in your mind. I've told you I'm going to help. And we're going to see that you get some help from the relief."

The relief had already been down there, and she had told the caseworker that she was going to give the children up for adoption. "We'll call the caseworker back."

"I know it's a tough decision. I know it is. If you were sixteen years old? I could see it, but not at 34. Pa won't rest in peace. Mama is still alive, and she wouldn't want it either."

So we decided to bring the children home.

Vera called Bill. He said he was going to bring some clothes for them to wear home. But he didn't show up.

I told Red Lucy that I was going down to the hospital to get Vera and the children. Red Lucy and her husband would do what they could to help Vera. But they didn't have anything, because they were on the relief, too. One of the other roomers in the apartment gave me ten dollars. She's the one that named the babies.

So I went to pick the children up. Not a stitch to put on them. Everything they had on was hospital clothes. I didn't have enough of Wendy's clothes to share with them. I really didn't have any money. Standard Brands would be paying me every two weeks.

Since it was August, I asked the nurses there if they would just put their little shirts on and wrap them in a receiving blanket. I'd share with them what we had. We could wash one shirt, put it on them, and wash another.

The nurses all chipped in to buy the babies some clothes. They went downstairs and got Nina a yellow outfit and Nelson something to wear.

The nurses gave me a sterilizer for the bottles. They gave me all the bottles, 24 diapers, and two receiving blankets.

I didn't have a bed to put them in, but I knew Vera couldn't sleep in the bed with the babies. She just had a room and a kitchenette where she was living. There was a chest of drawers in her room. I took the two drawers out of it, hung a sheet over the chest of drawers, and sat them on top of the chest of drawers, so mice couldn't get in.

I had four pillows. I took two pillows and put one in each drawer. I folded up some material and put it under there for a little pillow. Then I took a sheet that I had and cut it in half. I had a tablecloth that somebody had given me, and I cut that up. That's how I made some little sheets for the babies' beds until we could get something.

It was just about a week that I went backwards and forth. I thanked God I got the babies home. I didn't know whether Vera was pleased or whether she wasn't.

I'd come home and cook the food. I'd take her dinner uptown to the room she rented. I had stuff already there for her so she could have some breakfast when she woke up.

That Sunday I'd baked a half a ham and took it up there. And there lay Bill in that bed. I was hurt. I was just hurt that he had put her aside, thrown the children away, and put her through that much torture. It was torture for her, and for me.

I left the food for them. I didn't take it back home. I don't have that kind of heart. But I didn't cook any more food and take it up there to her. I said to myself, "If she's going to sit there and not let him feed her, then she'll starve to death." Now that Vera was going to be on the relief, I guess that's when Bill decided to move in.

I didn't go back up there on Monday. One of the women who lived in her rooming house helped Vera to bring the babies downtown to see me on Tuesday. The relief had given her a crib.

I put the babies on PET Evaporated Milk. I bought them the first case of milk they ever had; it was cheaper by the case. They didn't nurse at all. So they used a lot of milk. And that's what started those children off.

After Nina and Nelson were born, Vera didn't have a job, so there wasn't any money to send down south. She hadn't been sending that much anyway, but now there wasn't any for her sons, Ken, Ben, and Steve, which meant when my youngest sister, Nora, didn't have any money, she got in touch with me. I would have to send her money so they could get some food.

In October or November Vera did some part-time domestic work up in the Bronx while a blind lady took care of the twins. Her small salary helped a little down south.

It was 1954. My youngest sister, Nora, had taken Wendy back down south with her after the Fourth of

July. But I wanted Wendy home for New Year's 1955. I had let her stay down south long enough. I wanted Big Ma to come, too. In order to get Big Ma, I had to send for my youngest brother, Calvin, too. Big Ma couldn't come by herself on the train with Wendy. My sisters down there said Calvin wasn't going to come. Nora was going to come in his place, which meant I would've had to send her back, because she had to go back to her job.

Vera said Big Ma wasn't coming. "You're not going to get that child unless you go down there."

"When that train leaves Greenville, South Carolina, Big Ma better be on it with my child."

"She can't leave my other children down there."

"I have nothing to do with your children down there. But when that train leaves Greenville, South Carolina, Big Ma better be on that train. I've sent her the ticket. She can go back the next day. It's all right with me. Just bring my child home."

Sure enough, Big Ma and Calvin were on the train. He almost missed it because he was out trying to get some joy juice.

Now I had to try to find Calvin a job. My cousin, Dorothy, was nice about that. She knew about an opening in a butter factory in New Jersey. I didn't have a phone, so she sent one of her friends down to the house to tell me where to take Calvin the next morning.

I had to make the coffee and make breakfast, because Big Ma had never done anything for herself, and Sally wouldn't do it either. Then I had to walk Calvin up to my cousin's house so the man could take him to see about the job. Doing all this made me a little late for work. Calvin did get the job.

When Vera and Calvin were living down south, I wanted to know where was their money going? Nora was in school, but Vera and Calvin were working. So what were they doing, the two of them, that they couldn't pay the water bill and the light bill and eat? I was paying the mortgage. They couldn't pay the other bills?

I'll tell you the story of how Vera got here. I wanted her to come north to work to make money to fix the house in Greenville, South Carolina. That's how Sally and Vera both got here.

Then when they got here, to my surprise, nobody was gonna do anything. They weren't gonna even work to take care of themselves! I was supposed to take care of them down south and up here, too.

It didn't work out. It was a nightmare, and still haunts me. Because sometimes I feel like if I hadn't brought

Vera here, she would have been there down south with her other children. And maybe they wouldn't have gotten into drugs and alcohol.

I had no help. It was just a . . . nightmare, nightmare, *nightmare*. It looked like everything anybody could put on you, they just put on you. I guess it made me stronger. But the most important thing was I had a roof and I had a job.

I don't think it was the financial part that bothered me most. . . . It was actually the time that had to be used for somebody else when I could have used it for myself.

It did affect my life in a lot of ways, but I still don't think it affected my marriage. I think the marriage had problems from the beginning.

I really never had time to try to solve what was going on with me because there was always some kind of family crisis. It seems as though I was the one who was supposed to solve it, because it was put at my doorstep, so I had to try to figure out what to do with it. But then when I got it solved . . . I seemed to be the person who they wanted to fault for the problem being there in the first place.

I'm sure it started from childhood. I was the one to speak up, especially when we were in a business situation.

I do remember one incident. We went to a lady; we were living on her place, and she wanted us to pick berries.

We were under the impression that she was going to pay us for them.

I wanted to take the money and get us some material so we could make us some clothes. I don't know what Calvin was going to do with his dime. We might have got enough money to make him a shirt.

She decided she wasn't going to give us any money; she was going to give us hats. She was going to give ten-year-old Calvin one of her son's shirts, which was a nightshirt for him because it hung all the way down to his legs.

When she got to me—I don't know what she said she was going to give me, but I told her no. She couldn't give me anything, because I wanted the money. We needed some dresses because we had to go to summer school for six weeks.

She said no, she wasn't going to give me the money, because she had told our father that she had some things.

"All right, then you don't get my blackberries." So I took my blackberries back home.

Vera had the hat and it blew apart before she got home. Calvin's shirt—Daddy probably wore it. But it was rotten; her stuff was old. I must have been 11 or 12 years old; it was 1932.

When she saw my father she said to him—they called everybody "gal"—"One of them little gals of yours, I don't know what you going to do with her. She wouldn't let me have the blackberries because I didn't give her the money."

Daddy said, "I gave her the dime for the blackberries. She needed material for a dress. That's what she wanted."

"I don't know what she—"

"No, I don't have to worry about her. She'll be all right."

Because I didn't do what the rest of them did, I guess she thought they should have spanked me because there was something wrong with me.

I bought some cloth to make me a dress. But Vera didn't have a new dress. I told them they didn't have to let the lady have the basket of blackberries either. But I guess they were afraid.

I think Vera was the one who was supposed to speak up, because she was the oldest. But she never took the initiative. So I always took the lead. Then when I grew up, I found myself in the same situation, which I didn't want to be in.

My mother, too, would always say, "You know you have to do such and such for so-and-so." If I didn't help them, something would be wrong with me. I guess she just wanted each child to have what he or she needed.

Two of the things I did after I was grown—I still fault myself—was letting them all come to Greenville and buying the house so everybody could live there, and bringing them to New York. I shouldn't have done that.

If I hadn't, I would have been able to do the things that I wanted to do for myself in life. I wouldn't have had to make sure that this one had a job or that one had something.

I guess throughout all the pain and all the grief, I came out ahead of all the rest because I have my daughter. That's the only thing I can say. I have Wendy as a human being. I haven't seen any one of them that was a human being, out of all the sisters and all the nieces and the nephews and the greats and the grands. They don't understand me; and they don't understand Wendy.

They said I was mean, growing Wendy up. But I know I wasn't mean, so it doesn't bother me. I just had standards and we had goals in life. And we reached for those goals.

I had to fight all the way to get Wendy what I wanted her to have, because they thought I shouldn't send her to private school. They felt Wendy should be in public school so I could give the extra money to them.

I started cutting back on doing things for my sisters and brothers. I cut back as much as I could. But some things I just couldn't cut back on, because it was put at my door. Like Vera, Bill, Nina, and Nelson—they were eight years old then—coming to live with us when she was put out of her apartment.

These things are just dropped on you. You just . . . have to share those burdens. I had always been the dumping ground for all of them. Now, what they don't understand is that I'm . . . letting it a loose.

Life has its ups and it has its downs. One thing, you can't go back and pull back time, but you can stop and say this is enough. I do know that my family did affect my goals in life.

I said I was going to school. That was my plan when I came to New York. But then other things kept getting in my way. I said, "Let me take care of all these other things," which was the family. The more money I poured in, I still didn't get any good results. But thank God that my daughter came along and I knew I had something that I had to do something for, and that was Wendy.

CHAPTER 6

GETTING THE APARTMENT

Relegated to the jobs with the lowest salaries, colored people were then compelled by racially segregated housing to pay the highest rents. According to the U.S. Census Bureau, in 1950 the median gross monthly rent for an apartment in the metropolitan area of New York City, which included New Jersey, was $48.30. My mother was paying $100 a month for a room.

Our room was $25 a week for the three of us when Len was there, and stayed the same after he left. It was $30 for the large room in the back and $15 for the little room. I don't remember all the others. But it was enough for the landlady to make at least $250 a month off of the apartment. She only paid $54.10 a month for rent, and she paid the gas and light bill. There were a lot of people who were able to get homes out in Long Island or the Bronx by doing this.

When I first went there, Mrs. Troutman didn't want to give me a receipt.

I told her, "In every five and ten-cent store, whatever you buy, they give you a receipt." So she gave me a receipt. I did have proof that we were paying her. After she had to give me receipts, she had to give everybody receipts.

I had to accept the situation, because at that particular time—you're talking about 1953—there were no apartments available in Harlem. And if there were, it wasn't the landlord that didn't want children in the apartments; it was the people who were subletting these apartments who didn't want them.

I used to clean John Gambling Senior and his wife's apartment when I was at Taylor Maid. After I left Taylor Maid—and was working full-time at Standard Brands—I would go on the weekend to cook for them. They were out in Massapequa then. WOR, where he was broadcasting from, was around Sixth Avenue in the Columbus Circle area. I used to leave work and meet him there. And Mrs. Cahan would call me to do special parties for her. That's how I was able to pay that $25 a week.

The landlady, Mrs. Troutman, seemed to be a warm person at first. When Mrs. Troutman went to Kansas City on vacation in June or July of 1953, she sent Wendy and me a card. It was the first card Wendy received in her own name.

Then she rented a room to a lady with a dog. That's when she began to get annoyed with me. I didn't think it was healthy to have a dog fastened up in the house with a baby. The dog was all over the house, but they just had a room.

The young woman who owned the dog was named Lucy, but we called her Red Lucy. The other one who lived in the apartment was called Black Lucy. Red Lucy had a husband named Ralph. She could understand my not wanting the dog in the house. Red Lucy told me she'd take the dog back where it came from. It was her cousin's dog.

But Mrs. Troutman asked me to move. I started looking for someplace to go. But there weren't any places to be had. When I told her I couldn't move, she stopped taking the rent. I said, "I don't know what I'm going to do."

This was in August during the time that Len went down to Atlantic City for two weeks after he hit me. Ralph said to me—I really didn't know too much about housing or anything, because I had never rented an apartment in New York City—that he knew where the housing department was for Harlem. Ralph said he would go up there and report it; it wasn't legal for her to have the apartment rented out as rooms.

I had gone to Hulan Jack to see about it, because I knew his brother-in-law. He told me I should be satisfied with having a room. Just pay the lady what she asked. I knew then he wasn't going to help me. Hulan Jack was the councilman of this area then. He wasn't the borough president yet.

Ralph went to the housing department at 145th Street. He reported what was going on in the building and how much everybody was paying for rent. As the roomers moved out, they gave me their receipts.

After Ralph reported it, the housing department sent Mrs. Troutman a statement listing what the rent should have been. I should have been paying $9 a week. And the other folks, some of them should have been paying $4 and some should have been paying $3 if she was going to rent it out as rooms.

When she got this notice that the rent was being cut, she stopped taking the rent. The housing department told me to send her a registered letter first. If she sent that back, the department said don't bother to send the rent anymore. This was to show that I had offered it to her and she wouldn't take it.

This was all behind the landlord's back. The agent came to collect the rent, but most of the time the rent was mailed in. Then the housing people reported it to the landlord.

I asked Mrs. Troutman to go down to the agency and tell them that I was her niece, to see if they would let me have the apartment. She told me no.

I thought, "We'll just stay here. If they're going to put us in the street, we'll open up a manhole and go in it." By this time, Len had left.

In the meantime, Mr. Dillon, the owner of the building and the real landlord, contacted me. He told me to come down to his office on Columbus Avenue in the 90s.

"I heard you took Mrs. Troutman's apartment," he said.

"How could I take Mrs. Troutman's apartment? If Mrs. Troutman had been living there, I wouldn't be there. I guess you don't know what goes on in your own building, do you?"

"She just said she had to move out because of you."

"What would I be doing there in the first place? Okay, let's start from the beginning. I was renting a room from Mrs. Troutman. Mrs. Troutman does not live there. She has not lived there in a number of years. Mrs. Troutman had every room rented out except the bathroom and the kitchen.

"Here is the information. You know how many rooms are in the apartment? I have a receipt for every room."

"Where does Mrs. Troutman live?"

"I don't know exactly what the address is, but she bought a two-family house up in the Bronx and has been there for quite some time."

He sat back there behind the desk, a very tall man. After I got to know him, I found out he was a fine person, a fair person.

"What do you want?"

"I'd like to get the apartment for me and my daughter."

"Mrs. Troutman told me you were a prostitute and you took numbers."

"If a number taker and a prostitute is a working woman, I'm it. Here's three telephone numbers. Call them and see if they don't know Josephine Ebaugh Jones. They'll tell you what I do. I work for Standard Brands—that's my regular job. I was hired there in September. I have two other jobs that I work part-time."

"There ain't a room in Harlem worth $25 a week," he laughed. "You sure this is—"

"This is a receipt. This is not my handwriting. This is her handwriting."

"All right."

"There's nobody there now but me and my baby." Everybody else was gone, because they got frightened. Folks like Red Lucy ran because they were on the relief. Ralph wasn't supposed to be living there. The people back there in that large room—they weren't married then, but they were using the name Mr. and Mrs. Simon—left so I could have some place for the baby.

Mr. Dillon said, "She says you are not with your husband."

"That's right. My husband is gone. But you know what? I don't know whether you got your right wife. And I know Mrs. Troutman doesn't have her first husband, because he's dead. Mrs. Troutman doesn't know anything about me.

"My husband and I are separated; but that's life, and we must move on. I have to have a place for my baby. If I didn't have the baby, I'd be gone. That's why I'm fighting.

"I am going to keep my child. Mrs. Troutman said for me to send my child down south, but my mother didn't give birth to this child. She's mine, and I'm going to keep her. I'm going to make a home for us."

"All right, you go on back home and you'll hear from me in a couple of days. Good luck to you."

In a couple of days, his agent came by. He said I had to pay two months' rent and give him $75 under the table. The housing people were keeping in contact with me. They told me to give him the money. They gave me marked money for him if he asked for under-the-table money. He wasn't supposed to be accepting any bribes, because he was getting paid to do that job. Two weeks after that, he didn't have a job. Mr. Dillon fired the agent and started collecting his own rent.

In the meantime, before we were able to get the apartment, Mrs. Troutman had a sister who lived in that building. Mrs. Troutman wanted her sister's brother-in-law to take the apartment. This happened on a Sunday in the winter. I had finally found a part-time job where I could leave from Standard Brands and go to work. My employer was a lawyer.

I came home that evening and there were all these people standing there. Mrs. Troutman still had the key. They were going to give me the small bedroom in the back. They were going to take the front rooms until I could find someplace to go.

"Mrs. Troutman can't rent this apartment. This apartment belongs to Mr. Dillon."

I called the lawyer I was working for. He told me I was entitled to the apartment.

I was frightened, because Vera and the twins, Nina and Nelson, usually came down and stayed on the weekends with us, so they were there. But they were going home, so that wasn't going to leave anybody but Wendy and me. I went to see Red Lucy. She and Ralph said they would come spend the night with us.

I went out on the street and found a cop. I was telling him about the predicament I was in and that I was afraid. They had a key and I didn't know when they'd come in. I might come back and not be able to get in. He asked me if I had any furniture in there. I told him I did. Then he asked me if I had any money and did I have to go to work. I told him I did have to go to work and I did have some money.

"Tomorrow see if you can go to work and get off early. Come back and get Kingfish [the locksmith] to change that lock on that door. You have the authority to do that. Don't sleep in that house with two keys out somewhere."

"She can't do anything?"

"No, you got furniture in there."

So I went to work. I told Miss Sommers that I wanted to leave just after lunch. After everybody ate, I cleaned up and left. I went up to Kingfish on Lenox Avenue. I did not trust him to come by himself. He walked on back down there with me and changed the lock on the door.

Then I went back to the cop and asked him about the gas. They had turned the lights off. Con Edison did come to turn the gas off, but in the end they wouldn't turn it off, because Wendy was a baby and she had to have her formula.

Again, he asked me if I had any money. I don't know whether he was going to lend me some money or what. He was a young, black cop. I told him yes, I had some money. He said, "You go to Con Edison and have the lights put on in your name." He said the law couldn't do anything to me because I had to fix a home for me and the baby.

So that next evening I went down to Con Edison after work to have the lights changed over into my name. I didn't know about the office at 125th Street. I went down to No. 4 Irving Place. They told me there was a lot owed on the bill.

"As soon as we find out where she is, we will get the money from her. Then we will credit your account. But you have to agree to pay the balance. Pay down on it till you get it paid up. If she's still in Manhattan and paying a light bill, we'll find her record. That's just the law."

I agreed to it because I had to have the lights back on.

She was leasing a house on 119th Street, so they found her. Yeah, Mrs. Troutman was a business lady; she was raking it in.

When we got the lights, gas, and everything on, we were in business. Mrs. Troutman came out there the next morning before I went to work and tried to put her key in the door.

Key didn't fit that lock! I heard her out there scrimmaging and going on. I didn't want to come out there with her in the hall, because she was big.

I waited until I heard her going upstairs to her sister on the sixth floor. We were on the fourth floor. I came on out and went to work.

We didn't have a telephone. So she wrote a note and put it under the door. She said she wanted me out of there. Why did I have the lock changed? I had her phone number, but I didn't call her.

I called Mr. Dillon and told him what I done. He said, "That's good. Your home is your castle. You're entitled to it. I'll get somebody around to see about the lease."

In the meantime, these cousins of mine, who had money and could have lent us money or offered some help, didn't offer us anything.

My cousin Dorothy's son had said, "Well, you didn't get the apartment." He said a Mr. Williams, who lived on the second floor, was going to get the apartment because he had the money to pay for it.

"You wanna bet? Mr. Williams gonna stay where he is. I'm going to get this place."

"They said you didn't have enough—"

"Ain't nobody said nothing to me about money."

Mr. Dillon had just told me to sit still. I had enough faith and enough confidence in the law that they wouldn't sit my baby and me out.

True enough, they did come the next week with the lease. That's when Wendy's grandfather, her father's father, died. That same Saturday I gave Mr. Dillon one month's rent, which was $54.10. I gave him everything I had except carfare. Mr. Dillon wanted me to give the super $25. I told him I just didn't have it. I'd try to give Pops something later. We had to eat and I had to go to work. I wouldn't get paid until the end of the month. That was Saturday the 19th of June in 1954. That was the day we finally got the apartment.

By that time, Nora, my youngest sister, had come to New York. I sent for Nora to take care of Wendy. Sally had been sick, but she was better then. Sally wouldn't take care of Wendy even though she had a job cleaning at night.

Just after the landlord had got all I had, Wendy's father, Len, came by and rang the bell. He showed me the telegram saying that his father had died that day. Wendy's grandfather had been up to see us on the Fourth of July. He came and held her. Wendy's name still hadn't been put on the birth certificate. He told Len to "stop all this foolishness" about Wendy's name and sign the certificate. And the next year, he was dead.

Len wanted to go to the funeral, but he said he didn't have any money. I didn't have any money to give him. Maybe I would have given it to him if I had had it.

Nora, who was almost 19, came up here and stayed to help take care of Wendy, because Sally was sick. When Nora went back home to Greenville after the Fourth of July in 1954, she carried Wendy back with her. I had to have the money to get the ticket for Nora and pay the rent.

Luckily, Mrs. Cahan or Taylor Maid gave me a day's work to do that week, so we made it all right. I had the apartment, but I didn't have much furniture, no more than just a bed, a table, and two chairs. Mrs. Troutman didn't leave any furniture in the house. Mrs. Cahan had given Wendy a youth bed. We put it up and one of my sisters slept on it.

But I was so thankful that I had this lease. I had the lease! I had what it took to stabilize our life. I didn't have to look back.

I said to myself, "I'll just sit here until I get the down payment and I'll get some more furniture." At that time you got the furniture on credit, and you paid by the month or by the week. But I paid by the month. I never liked to pay anything weekly. It was ten or fifteen dollars a month. After you paid so much down, they delivered it. I went to Maxwell House, down on 34th Street, to get the furniture. That was a week before Christmas.

I bought a living room suite, a bedroom suite, and some lamps and tables. I had at least two or maybe three years to pay the furniture off. We didn't have any rugs on the floor, but it was scrubbed and clean. We shellacked it because we couldn't have it scraped.

I asked my cousin Ravena would she let her husband paint some for me. No, her husband wasn't coming down there to paint anything for me. People who were in a position to help me did not. They just wanted to see you broken down. I offered to buy the paint for him, but she still said no.

I don't know why I didn't paint it myself. We whitewashed when I was growing up, but I was afraid I'd mess up the wall. It was a burgundy red wall.

Instead of painting, we washed the woodwork, the windows, and the floor. Sometimes Sally would help and sometimes she wouldn't; mostly, it was me. She had some male friends that would come and help. Sometimes Ralph and Red Lucy, my friends, the former roomers, would come by and give me a hand.

Mostly Red Lucy took care of Wendy's clothes. I'd wash them and she ironed them. She said I couldn't iron to suit her. Nothing that Red Lucy and Ralph did, did they charge me for.

I was able to wash and do all these things for the apartment because Wendy was still down south with my sister, Nora. Sally wasn't working either. And where was Vera? Vera had Nina and Nelson. This was '54. Vera would come help me scrub and get the things together.

CHAPTER 7

CREATING A CAREER

Founded in June 1929, just four months before the beginning of the Great Depression, Standard Brands was a combination of three companies: Chase & Sanborn Coffee, Royal Baking Powder (premixed cream of tartar and baking soda to make baked goods rise), and Fleischmann and Co., which made yeast. Chase & Sanborn and Royal were founded in 1863, while Fleischmann was established in 1868.

By 1953, Standard Brands sold Chase & Sanborn Coffee, Tenderleaf Tea, Royal puddings, gelatin, and tapioca, in addition to Royal Baking Powder. The Fleischmann's division made "Black & White" Scotch as well as Fleischmann's Yeast.

This Fortune 500 company subsidized the cafeteria as one of the employees' benefits. Standard Brands charged for sandwiches and cake, but they provided their own Chase & Sanborn Coffee for free.

Although my mother originally went to work for only two weeks as a summer replacement in the employees' cafeteria at Standard Brands' national headquarters in midtown Manhattan, she ended up staying 31 years. She had been highly recommended by Mr. Taylor, of Taylor Maid, the agency she worked for as a temporary maid and later as a cook in private homes.

I first went to Standard Brands as a temp in August of 1953. I was just getting ready to leave the book factory, because my sister Vera had given birth to twins, Nina and Nelson, in August. My sister had been looking after Wendy for me, so I was going to have to stop working. I got to Standard Brands through Taylor Maid. Mr. Taylor wanted me to represent Taylor Maid on this job, so he gave me money to pay one of the roomers to take care of the baby.

I went in on a Monday at eight o'clock. I was originally supposed to work just two weeks. They had already hired somebody in place of the person who was retiring. But I could see that the one that they had hired and the one that was already there would not be able to do the job.

The supervisor told me that she was sorry that they had hired somebody else. She asked me if I had worked there before. I told her no, but this was my line of work. I could do it in any situation I came into. In two weeks' time the employees were attached to me.

Management asked me to stay an extra week with the ladies to see if I could train them. But they were people who really didn't want any supervision from me. The people I was training were both white. They were not able to work on their own and neither was anybody from management able to supervise them. It was a food company, but not a restaurant operation, so they didn't know how to operate the cafeteria.

You didn't have to cook; you just had to know how to set up the sandwiches that came from Schrafft's restaurant. We just had sandwiches, coffee, tea, drinks, and cake. All of it came in a box. It had to be taken out of the box and the price tag and the sandwich label put on the items; for instance, ham and swiss for thirty-five cents. Then you put the sandwiches on separate trays.

These were the things that they couldn't organize. They'd get the sandwiches mixed up. Schrafft's used the crates that the eggs came in to pack the sandwiches in. They came in a huge box that held thirty-two dozen with a layer of paper in between to say which was which.

The cafeteria staff didn't realize that the paper underneath the sandwiches was the one that had the name on it. They thought the name on the top should have the name of the sandwiches. So they'd get them all mixed up. They didn't even bother to listen because I was in charge. One of them had been there four or five years, so she was sure she knew what to do, but she didn't.

I left, and said to myself, "If this place operates, you'll get me or somebody else, but it won't be these two."

I'd been home about two weeks—the phone rang. It was Mr. Taylor.

"Ebaugh"—he still called me by my maiden name—"I got good news for you. Standard Brands wants you permanent. They want you to come back down there so you can take the physical exam. The other people they had are not working out."

"Mr. Taylor, they don't pay enough money. They're just paying forty-five dollars a week, and you get paid every two weeks." When I did dinner parties, I would make that much in one *night*. The people always tipped me very, very well.

"You go there and you can still do dinner parties for me. But I want you to take that job. Listen, you are a young mother and you'll need the benefits. My company can never give you the benefits they have. It's an old reliable company. Go there and take that job. They want you, so ask them for more money in the beginning. Just tell them that you can't stand a cut in salary."

So I said all right. It was the weekend before Labor Day. I went back down there that Friday to take the physical. I asked for more money then, but they said they'd look at me in thirty to sixty days and see if I could get more. Then before the ninety days were up, they did look at me and gave me ten dollars a week increase.

From the beginning, I was having trouble with the counterperson that they kept. Anita was afraid to make decisions. If I was left on my own to make a decision, I would use my best judgment. If you told me what to do, I would follow your instructions.

Anita started complaining to the supervisor that I would always make a decision. I'd sign when people came in to bring the products. They had given me that authority.

When it was time to go home, I'd have all the receipts and take them out to the supervisor so she could put them in the file.

After Anita complained about that, the supervisor told her that was my responsibility. She couldn't come out there and count the products every morning. In fact, most of the time when the order arrived, Mrs. Sommers wasn't even in the office.

I would try to get there a little earlier so I could get a head start. Whew! I have never seen water take so long to get hot. We had to have the coffee ready by the time the people came in. They must have drunk about fifty gallons of coffee. I had never seen anybody drink as much coffee as those folks were drinking. I didn't know whether it was because it was free or because they really needed it.

I think we worked from eight to three then. Anita came in at six o'clock, but lots of times I'd get there at eight o'clock and she'd just be turning the water on. It wouldn't be ready by nine. She was trying to get me fired. I'd try to get there by seven-thirty so I could give the water a half an hour longer to heat. Anita complained about my coming in early. I wasn't getting any more money for it, but I wanted the coffee to be ready on time.

It was an electric urn that held five gallons. I had tried to get management to let me leave it on low at night. But they didn't want to do that. We had to start it off with warm water. In fact, coffee is supposed to be started off with cold water.

The supervisor said, "Jo's coming in on her own time. That benefits her, so just leave her alone."

That didn't sit well with Anita; she didn't win on that.

Finally, she said to me one day—she was Italian and spoke with an accent, "Are you permanent?"

"What do you mean?"

"Are you permanent?"

"I don't understand what you're talking about."

"Are you here to stay?"

"We all are here to stay. I'm here to stay and you're here to stay, too."

Anita didn't understand that the company had hired me.

"You got a baby?"

"Yes, I got a daughter."

"Why don't you stay home and take care of her and go on the relief?"

"Are you kidding? I've got a job. I don't have to go on the relief. We just need two people working." Wendy's father and I hadn't separated then. "Why is it bothering you that I'm working? You're not paying me."

"I just thought you ought to stay home."

"I'm not staying home. I'm going to work. My child is very well taken care of."

She let that go.

I guess Anita said to herself, "Now I got to do something else. I got to get her fired."

We had the old-fashioned sugar shakers, which held about a pint of sugar and had an open top with a hole in it that let out however much you wanted. You could measure it if you wanted to or you could dump it out. We also had saltshakers; it was my responsibility to wipe the tables down and to fill the saltshakers and the sugar shakers.

I found an old stainless steel coffee pot, washed it out, scrubbed it up with Brillo, and dried it on the heat. I let it sit around for two or three days until all the moisture was out of it so the sugar wouldn't get damp when I put it in there. There was a 25-pound bag of sugar that the staff had been dipping sugar out of with a cup and filling the sugar shakers with it. The salt came in consumer-size boxes.

If I filled the sugar on one day, then I filled the salt the next day. We had about fifty tables in there. We looked around and the salt was getting over into the sugar. So I was puzzled. I knew I had only filled it with sugar. I knew I was putting sugar in the sugar shaker. I knew it.

I'd handled them both; throughout my lifetime, I'd handled almost all aspects of food. I could tell the difference between the grains of sugar and salt. The salt is coarse and the sugar is very fine. If I were blind, I could tell the difference.

In the morning, we sent the coffee around. But at lunchtime, the employees said, "Jo, this coffee tastes like it has salt in it."

I tasted the coffee and it was salty. I tasted the sugar and it had some salt in it, but I didn't know where it was coming from. We took up all the sugars off the table, got some containers, and put some sugar in them for that particular day. That evening I stayed late. We emptied out every sugar shaker that was supposed to have salt in it. Not every table had salt in the sugar. We tested it all.

I told Mrs. Sommers, "Let's dump them all." I washed them all out and I turned them down. We put the dishwasher on dry. We didn't fill them that night. We waited till the next morning to fill them, which meant it was going to carry over into the next night. That lunchtime there was no salt in the sugar because we filled the saltshakers that morning.

But the next morning when they came in to lunch, there was salt in the sugar again. Mrs. Sommers said to me, "I don't know what it is, but there's something wrong around here. I know we didn't put any salt in these sugar shakers."

I said, "Somebody is doing it at night. The people putting the salt in the sugar shakers are taking it out of the salt shakers. I can tell the difference in the morning. The employees don't use this much salt."

"We are going to have to find out what's going on, Jo. We can't keep doing this. It's just too much."

One of our Standard Brands men worked from four to twelve; he was our night watchman. He was supposed to see that the cleaning people from National didn't steal our stuff at night. The night watchman hid out on Halloween night to catch the witch.

In the storeroom, he was locked up in a place where he could look out over the dining room. She didn't know that he was watching her when she did it. He told Mrs. Sommers that he had found the missing link.

One of Anita's friends was cleaning the dining room for National from six to ten at night; she was the one who was doing it. Anita wanted her to have my job. See, it was more of a prestigious job than cleaning. Mrs. Sommers and management went to National. I don't think they fired her, but there wasn't any more salt in the sugar.

I don't think they ever confronted Anita, but I'm sure she found out through her friend. They were doing that trying to get me fired, but it worked in my favor.

Then Anita stopped speaking to me for two or three days. I said to myself, "It doesn't bother me whether she speaks or not." I spoke when I came in.

Mainly her job was to take care of the executive suites in the morning. She would fill their thermoses with water, take coffee up to the ones that needed coffee, and see if their bathrooms were clean.

My job was to get the coffee ready for these people. They didn't have anybody taking the coffee around like they did when Wendy came down there to work during the summer. The guys would come down and get their jugs and the girls would fill their thermoses and take them back up to their floors.

I had to have enough of it there to keep them supplied and keep the water hot. They had sugar shakers and napkins upstairs at their stations. We stopped serving coffee about 10:15. Then we got ready for lunch.

I was just going to do my work. And everybody else there was nice to me. When Anita retired, she still hadn't warmed up to me. But she left me alone and stopped having folks pick at me.

The people at the company finally found out that Wendy's father and I had separated. It was during January 1954 when the summons came from the hospital concerning the unpaid bill for the baby's birth. I went down to Maiden Lane to the lawyer's office to see if I could pay it monthly.

She was a white lawyer. I looked in her face and I guess she said to herself, "Here is another candidate for relief, so I guess I'll put her on the city rolls."

I still hadn't been there long enough to get that increase. I was still just making $45 a week and getting paid every two weeks. I told her I would give her $10 a month until I could get it paid. It was $150, but it sounded like $10,000 to me.

Her first words to me—television had just come out—was how many televisions did I have? I told her I didn't have any because I didn't watch television. I was not a movie person. I went to plays, but I picked the plays I went to.

"You can stay on the relief until your daughter is 12 years old. The city will pay the hospital bill."

"The city didn't father this child. There were nine of us, and my father didn't put us on the relief. He took care of us. I'm as much of a woman as he was a man. I will take care of my child. And I will not go on the relief."

And then I said, "I have given you the options of what I can do. You want it all. I don't have it, and I don't have any place to get it from. Whatever you have to do, you do it. If they send us to jail, I'll take the child. I have a good job, and I will not go on the relief."

"We are not going to take it like that."

About two weeks before that, Mrs. Sommers had said that the smile had gone from my face. She asked me what was wrong. Was everybody there nice to me? I said, "Yes, I see people." My father didn't teach us anything about color; we saw people. She asked if the baby was all right. And I said yes.

A week or so after that, they sent a garnishee on the job. I think it probably went to personnel, but it got back to my supervisor. Mrs. Young was the top supervisor of my department. Mrs. Sommers was my immediate supervisor.

Mrs. Young said to me, "We have to talk about this now. We just got this notice from the collection department of the Flower Fifth Avenue Hospital where the baby was born."

I told her what had happened with the lawyer. "I'll go to jail, but I'm not going on the relief."

"No, you don't have to go on the relief. You have a job. Don't get upset. It's out of my control now; it's a legal matter. You know Mr. Weigl?"

"No. I guess I know his face. I don't know anybody by that name."

"He's head of the legal department. Bring all your papers tomorrow. I'll call up and make an appointment with him. I told you when you came here, we were like a family. He'll handle it for you."

Mrs. Young had made an appointment for me with him just about the time that I got off. He could see that I was nervous, so he told his secretary to make me a cup of tea.

His first words to me were, "Jo, whether we're rich or whether we're poor, we've all had some problems. I've had mine. I've gone over these papers here, as you see. Now, what is the arrangement?"

I told him the arrangement I had tried to make with the hospital's lawyer.

"I have to pay somebody to take care of the baby, we have to have food, and I have to pay rent. I just have a room. I pay $25 a week for this room. I'm trying to get the whole apartment, but I don't have it yet."

"All right, I will call and tell her what you want her to do."

"I want her to take it like I asked her to take it."

"We'll see that she does. If you want me to pay it outright, I'll pay it. I'll send her the check today."

"That's not what I want. My father always told us to take care of our own responsibilities. This is my responsibility."

"Legally, you don't have to pay it, because it's in Wendy's father's name. But it will ruin your credit rating, and you will need that for you and for your daughter."

"That's what I was trying to save. My father always said that credit was better than gold."

"Your credit is good."

All my credit was in my maiden name.

"I will pay it, because it was a service given to me and my child."

He got on the phone and called the lawyer, "I don't understand. We are human beings. We are here to help people, not to destroy people. I will not sit here and allow you to destroy this young woman and her child. Why did you tell her to go on the relief? Flower Fifth Avenue Hospital does not need that money that badly.

"Legally, she has a right to pay it the way she can pay it. She'll send you that ten dollars. She is our valuable employee. I'm sending the papers with the payment agreement down by a registered messenger. Please, don't put anybody else through this. We are professional people. We don't have to do this."

So, that case was closed. I sent $10 for fifteen months to the lawyer until I got it paid.

Some people will reach out to you and help you when you need it. I found that to be true in that company. I also found it in the Cahan family, who had the daughter that Wendy was named for. They all reached out to help me. It wasn't money that I needed from them; it was encouragement. If I was trying to do something, I needed the legal way to get it done. I was always able to ask some of the lawyers at Standard Brands or ask Mr. Cahan which was the legal route to go.

I think the Internal Revenue people also said go on the relief. I was told four times to go on the relief, including Anita. The ring was bought at Busch Credit Company; the storeowner wanted me to go on the relief. I still couldn't understand what good the relief was going to do helping me to pay the store when the relief couldn't give me the money that I was making. If you paid Busch Credit Company, what were you going to live off of?

Relief was a way of destroying black people. I was lucky that I was older than the average person out here that was left with a child. But even if I had been young, I still would have had that same determination that this is mine. I take care of mine: that was my background. And

I have never liked to ask anybody to lend me anything except the bank.

I was still helping my family down south. I was still paying on a home that I bought down there for my mother. Every one of the sisters that came by this way, you had to send for them. You had to pay rent for them and feed them until they could get a job. So I just hadn't gotten myself in a position to go back to school.

The company moved up the street to the next block, 625 Madison Avenue in Manhattan. The food wasn't any good. Then they wanted me to do something with it. I told them we couldn't do anything with it unless we had control over it. We'd have to have our own equipment and make our own sandwiches. We already had our own products.

After the employees continued to complain about the food, I decided to go talk to Mr. Long, the facilities manager, and Ms. Granley, who was the supervisor of the cafeteria at that time.

Mr. Long said, "It can't be done."

"All things are possible. It can be done. I know what equipment we need. A layout man could come in here and make sure it would fit in this space. We need a bain-marie and refrigerators. We have a coffee urn, but we'll need a counter."

"We could go to the grocery store and get the food," Ms. Granley said.

"You don't go to the grocery store to get food for restaurants. You buy it wholesale. That's why we need a slicing machine. You slice the bologna, the cheese, the ham. Everything comes in bulk."

Mr. Long said, "Oh, I didn't know."

I found the restaurant people in the Yellow Pages that they called. Then they came to see about setting up.

All this time I'm thinking I'm going to be the supervisor. I didn't think they would bring somebody in over me, but they did. They brought Mrs. Dunfield in. I was heartbroken, but I knew I could not leave because it was a secure job and I really wanted to work with food.

The only thing I knew to do was to go back to school and get the credentials that I needed, which were a Hotel and Restaurant Management Certificate and a Nutrition Certificate. The hospitals and the food industry were wide open then. You could get a good job.

I went down to personnel and asked if I went back to school, would they pay for it.

"Oh, Jo, you'll always have a job here. What are you worried about?"

"I want to go back to school so I can grow, so I can learn more about what I'm doing. I don't understand how we use protein, carbohydrates, and fats in our body."

"You'll be all right, but there's no money for you."

This was in '61 . . . I believe we opened the new cafeteria in '57.

So I kind of played around and I still didn't go. But I was getting more disillusioned, because we'd hired more people. It wasn't the same atmosphere. I had always worked alone. I wasn't used to working with these cutthroat people, Sue and Lola. I was really unhappy.

After Gertrude—who was a former secretary from the Transportation Department who refused to retire, so she was made Mrs. Dunfield's assistant—came to the cafeteria, she found out that I did the menu planning. She started all the problems between me and the other cafeteria employees.

They had worked in restaurants, but they weren't used to handling cold food. There is so much difference in handling cold food and hot food. With cold food, you have to do so much more to it than you do with hot food for people to accept it, especially working in an employees' cafeteria where you feed the same people every day.

I could do it, make the food look appealing, but then I wasn't getting any credit for it. I don't care what you share with people—if you are able to do things that they can't do, they are still annoyed with you.

Gertrude felt that it was some kind of favoritism. But I made more money than the other cafeteria employees did because I had been there longer than they had. I also had more experience than they did. Maybe Mrs. Dunfield, who had access to all our salaries, told Gertrude what my salary was. She kept talking to the other co-workers until they all turned against me.

The other employees in the cafeteria complained to Mr. Long, who was Mrs. Dunfield's supervisor. One or two mornings I went in late because Wendy was sick. One time her nose was bleeding, and I had to wait until it stopped bleeding before I could take her to the babysitter.

I had tried to get them to put me on flextime. I wanted them to let me come in later when Wendy was going to school. But nothing worked, because the other employees kept saying that would be showing favoritism.

Mr. Long sat down and told them that I had taken care of the employees very well. At that particular time, I think I had been there about ten years. The company knew I had the child and that I had to take care of her. The other employees couldn't understand why I should get consideration when they didn't have it.

He told them that the company had never had any problem with anything that I did. If I was late, he would appreciate it if there would be nothing said about it, because he knew that it was for a legitimate reason.

Mr. Long said that if I was a couple of minutes or a half hour or so late, it was nothing for anybody to complain about, because he had watched me work. He said when I came in I could do more work in an hour than most of them could do all day.

A lot of afternoons, he would come upstairs to sit and watch me clean the tables. That was before that group of cafeteria employees came in. I had the wet cloth in my right hand and I'd wipe the table with that. In my left hand I had the dry cloth, and I'd dry what I'd just wiped with that.

He couldn't understand how I could work with both of my hands. Having grown up on the farm, I could work with both of my hands well. You had to pick cotton with both hands.

Then they started saying I had tuberculosis, because I was very thin. I weighed a hundred and one, maybe a hundred and two pounds. Nobody wanted to sit near me and nobody wanted me to touch anything.

I told them, "I get a checkup every year." I didn't have tuberculosis. I was thin because I didn't eat the kind of food that they ate and I didn't eat as much as they ate.

In the summertime, I'd take my lunch and go over to 59th Street on Columbus Circle. In the wintertime, I'd go to the back of the cafeteria and sit down and read the paper or a book and eat. It didn't bother me, because all the jobs I'd ever had, I was alone.

With some people, if you are able to survive in a situation that they couldn't survive in, they are always angry at you about it. If you can survive and you don't complain, there's something wrong with you. I had what I needed. I had a job; I had security. I didn't need anything from anybody.

I finally decided that I must go to school. I knew I had to go back to school, because I had to let Wendy see that I had accomplished something. In order to get out of that job and get something better, I had to have a degree in something. It had to be in food, because that's what I was going to work in.

In the past, you didn't have to have an education to get a job. Then came the time when you did have to have an education and experience, too. Higher learning for adults was just becoming popular, and you could borrow money. So I went down to Bowery Savings Bank on 42nd Street and Park Avenue underneath that bridge there, and I got the money I needed. You had to pay the money back after you graduated. You had to pay something down, but it wasn't that much. I believe the loan was nine hundred dollars. It wasn't that expensive like it is now.

Then I filled out the application I needed to get into school. I didn't have one minute's trouble. The school was the New York Institute of Dietetics (NYID), and Mrs. Manley was the director. That's how I lost my high school transcript. It wasn't like you could get copies of things like you can now. NYID promised to send my transcript back, but I never have been able to track it down. I had a great high school transcript.

I didn't have any trouble getting in and I didn't have any trouble once I got there in 1962. I was one of the few people that was working in food and wanted to further my education in it. The others were beauticians, nurses, and all. Some of them were just folks working in the factory. Some had never seen a professional kitchen. The school was just advertising that there was money to be made. If you graduated, the school would be responsible for getting you a job.

The length of the program was two and a half years. You received an associate's degree in dietetics. But within that course, you covered the chemistry part of food and nutrition. You had hotel and restaurant management. You had food purchasing; you had sanitation. You covered the food industry: the dietetics part of it, the business part of it, food costs and control. We had it all. It was a course that I did enjoy because it was what I was doing.

My younger sister, Sally, went around the neighborhood and said I'd never finish. Nobody gave me any encouragement. Cousin Dorothy had died the year before and I had taken in her roomer, Mazie, an older woman. She paid me $10 a week and cooked her own meals. I was lucky I had Mazie, so she would always be there with Wendy. I didn't go back to school until she was big enough to see about herself.

Classes were from 6 p.m. to 9 p.m., Monday through Thursday. We went summer and winter. We had Christmas vacation and Easter vacation, but it was for adults, so we just went straight through.

I met some nice people. It was fun to me. And I helped the other students—especially two students—to stay in school. I'd get on their case and call: "Come to school; you got to stay there." Flora and Lettie had no intention of finishing that course. They were much younger than

I was and didn't know the importance of when you start something, you finish it. We're still friends.

I liked the atmosphere of learning. After we got into the cooking class, we did hostess work as well as cooking. We had courses in hotel management and how to feed babies when they're sick, and nutrition in health and disease.

That's why I could do so much at Standard Brands, because I knew what to give the healthy folks and I knew what to give the sick folks. People who were on restricted diets at Standard Brands knew all they had to tell me was that they didn't eat salt. I even got salt-free bread for them. That's why I became such a special person at Standard Brands. That was one of the things that my co-workers didn't appreciate, about my being this special.

It came out very well. Wendy was there for the graduation. I received the food chemistry award and the attendance certificate. Mrs. Cahan had told me I wouldn't get the attendance certificate. But I got both. I showed her the chemistry award. I don't think she ever congratulated me, but that was all right.

I wouldn't stay and work for Mrs. Cahan on the nights when I had to go to school. I had always helped her with her dinner parties. I worked at 59th and Madison. She lived nearby. I'd just walk there and make dinner for her.

But when I had to go to school four nights a week, I couldn't do it. If she had had the dinner parties on Friday night, I could have done them, but she was determined not to have them on Friday nights, so I would have had to stay out of school.

When I graduated, I had calls from several hospitals. Joint Disease Hospital—it was still in operation then, over there on Madison Avenue on Mount Morris Park—called me. The Jewish Hospital up in the Bronx wanted me; Mount Sinai wanted me. I could have made great money, but I still don't regret it today, not going to the hospitals.

I wanted to stay where people were well, where I could make the food look attractive for them. I did create in a way that I wouldn't have been able to create in the hospital. I was able to do the culinary art part of food, the fruit carving, the vegetable carving, and the designing of food. Hospitals put the emphasis on the patient, but the patient could get well if he had the right food. But they won't put any emphasis on food; just medicine, and that's it.

It paid off. Wendy was somebody special at Standard Brands. She became the adopted child of that company. In the first part of our stay there, there was nobody there that didn't know her and nobody that didn't know me, so at Christmastime there were toys galore the first year.

Finally, I asked them to just give us the money; there were other places that we could utilize it that would benefit her more than toys. She couldn't play with but one toy at a time. I have never just bought Wendy a toy; I have always bought her books.

After the people at Standard Brands found out that Wendy's father and I were separated, they understood why I wanted the money. I would tell them what we did with it, whether we bought shoes or we used it for tuition.

I would always write them a thank-you note and tell them what part they played in our lives. I think they all appreciated that.

Now it turned out that Mrs. Dunfield had lied about her age. So she had to retire, and I was made supervisor of the cafeteria in 1967.

Our opening hour was 11:30. Lunch was from 11:30 until 2:00. The staff couldn't understand why I wanted to be ready at 11:30. One of the rules I learned when growing up was being on time, being reliable and responsible. That's lunch hour. You want it done right and on time.

There would be somebody out there waiting to get in. They wouldn't all be out there, because our cafeteria was not that large. We seated about two hundred and fifty people, but we had three hundred, and sometimes more, per day, which meant they themselves staggered their lunchtimes, eating in shifts.

They were a very good group of people. There was one group that came at 11:30, another that came at quarter to twelve, and a last group that came at twelve o'clock.

Most of our people didn't live in the city. The women wanted to go to Bloomingdale's and Alexander's, and the men usually took a walk. Some of the men played cards in the back of the cafeteria when they finished eating. They had to get back to that card game.

We didn't use china dishes; we used plastic, but we had the best of plastic. The utility person washed the pots and pans, kept the storeroom straight, packed the groceries, checked the groceries in and out, washed the fruits and vegetables, and put things away.

The first utility person that I really was able to train was Ron. Then he moved up to become the sandwich person. There was mobility for specific tasks and for different salary ranges, too. I made sure that the one who was more experienced was paid a higher salary.

In fact, I could have walked away from there whole if I had been the supervisor that some people were. By not giving my staff raises, I could have gotten a larger share of the budget for myself. But whenever I got an increase, they got an increase; I made sure they got the maximum.

One time it had been almost two years and we hadn't gotten an increase. We had changed supervisors. I didn't want to tell Mr. Weigl about it. I thought I should be able to handle my staff.

I asked Mr. Langley, who was in charge of personnel—my supervisor reported to him—if he knew what was going on. "It's going on two years and we haven't had an increase, we haven't had a salary review. It's not fair to me, and it's not fair to my staff. Do I have to go any higher than you? We work for Standard Brands, too."

"I didn't know you hadn't had one."

"Please let me know whether you can do it or not."

"I'll take care of it."

Miss Forbes was Mr. Langley's supervisor. She came over to talk to me. "I'll tell you what we'll do. We'll give you your retroactive increase, but we won't retroactive your staff's increase."

"No, Miss Forbes, that's not me. We all worked hard those days. We all have to get our retroactive salaries."

"That will be more for you."

"No, we'll all get our retroactive increase." And we did.

That's what happened to Lilly Manning, who worked for Rick Motley. That was why she was just making $135 a week when she left there. Motley, her supervisor, wouldn't give her the increases she was entitled to. She must have left sometime in '78.

She didn't know when she'd been given an increase. She kept pleading and begging for him to give her some kind of increase for the last five years, so her Social Security would be higher, but he wouldn't do it.

I told Francine, a former cafeteria staff member, not too long ago, they never knew what part I played. The former cafeteria employees refused to call me after they left. I don't have a guilty conscience. Whatever anybody else got in Standard Brands, my department was going to get.

Most people don't understand that you alone can't do all of this; you have to train other people to do it. People have to enjoy doing food. If they don't, you're not able to train them. From day to day, you're hoping that you have reached this person or that you can reach somebody else that you hire. You need to be a psychologist. You need to be a social worker. You need to be a teacher and you need to be a parent, too, when getting a staff together.

I ran across some good staff members, though you find most people are not interested in what they are doing. They have a job, and it's a livelihood. I tried to instill in them that they didn't have to keep this job. In the food trade, there are a lot of things that you can learn to do that you can be a specialist in. Food is one of the most lucrative fields there is, because people always have to eat, so there are always going to be some jobs around.

But it isn't easy to assemble a staff that is looking for the same product that you are looking for. That's the only thing about food that I don't want any more parts of, having to depend on somebody else to get something done.

Dr. Minnelli was head of research and development, developing products for Standard Brands. He said he was sorry, but they had wasted me. I should have never been in the cafeteria. I had more talent—dealing with food—than anybody he had ever seen, even someone with a PhD degree.

A few years later, our test kitchen went up to Stamford, Connecticut. Employees came from all parts of the States and all parts of Europe to discuss the budget. I always had to fix the luncheons for the budget meetings.

When Mrs. Tyler, Mr. Weigl's secretary, gave me the itinerary, she listed the country these people came from. I would get the atlas and look up what food they imported from us. That would be what I would arrange their luncheon around. That was food that they really didn't have access to, because it was very expensive, like steaks. Steaks are expensive in Japan. Instead of giving them fish, you would give them steak.

I had stacks of letters of appreciation for luncheons that I'd served. I don't care how busy Mr. Weigl was, most of the time he penned me a note about the luncheon that I had served for them.

I'd always incorporate some of our products into the luncheon. Sometimes I'd put the gelatin in a honeydew and make it red and green like Christmas. I'd make the puddings, and sometimes I would put slices of Kiwi fruit on top of the vanilla instant pudding. I would put the custard in pre-baked custard cups. I was creative.

Dr. Minnelli had a meeting at Stamford with people from California. Mrs. Reynolds, head of the test kitchen, had the stoves and all the dieticians and access to all kinds of food. She served them a salad, soup, and sandwiches. And he hit the ceiling.

He told her, "If you can't do anything with food, you should go back down there to New York and see what Jo's doing with food. How could you serve my guests this kind of food?"

The next day Mrs. Reynolds was looking in my face. "We served Dr. Minnelli lunch last week, and he just ran all over us. What do you do with food?"

"Mrs. Reynolds, you know what I was doing with food when you left here. You know what kind of food I serve. I don't have a stove. All our food is cold."

"What do you do with the sandwiches?"

"Sandwiches? I just make a sandwich. There isn't but one way to make a sandwich."

But I wasn't going to tell her all that I did to the sandwich. Yes, I do something different besides putting a piece of meat between two pieces of bread in a sandwich. A lot of times it's how you cut it, how you present it to the person that makes it more appealing than just an ordinary sandwich.

"What did you serve, Mrs. Reynolds?"

"We had sandwiches, soup, and a salad."

"What kind of salad did you serve?"

"We had a mixed green salad."

"These people were from California?"

"Yes."

"Mrs. Reynolds, you should have known not to serve them salad. They got the best lettuce and tomatoes in the country. Never give folks what they got the best of. Give them something they can't get. That lettuce out there is crispy. They get it fresh from the farm."

Since they had a stove, they could have cooked. They should have made some broiled fish or chicken, had some fresh asparagus. And you wouldn't have had to worry about no salad. If I had had a stove, that's what I would have done. I wouldn't have been trying to fix anything cold.

I would have made a hot lunch if I had been in her position, had a dining room and everything that they had, and the cooks that they had. They didn't want to do anything to exert themselves, so they just made the same thing that they were giving the other people; it was easier for them.

"Well, I didn't know," said Mrs. Reynolds.

So she went on back up to Stamford. She didn't get too much information. That part of the company moved to Parsippany, New Jersey, when it became part of Nabisco. The test kitchen never did get back to New York.

When you make up a menu, it's just like you're writing a play. It's a three-act play that you're doing. It could go on stage.

CULINARY ART

5. CRENSHAW MELON

6. FRUIT BOWL

163

7. APPLE BIRDS

8. HAM WITH RICE AND CHAUDFROID SAUCE

9. SANDWICHES WITH VEGETABLES

10. GELATIN AND CAKE

11. SHRIMP WITH DIPPING SAUCE

12. NOT-A-CAKE SANDWICH LOAF

13. VEGETABLE SALAD FIXINGS

**14. PINEAPPLE WITH HONEYDEW MELON
AND WATERMELON**

CHAPTER 8

BEING INVOLVED WITH CHILDREN

The block that Mama and I lived on was a busy one-way street that was a quick way to get from Seventh Avenue to Lenox. There were no designated play streets closed to traffic in those days. During the steamy summers with only fans to push the muggy air around, most children played in the cooling spray of illegally turned-on fire hydrants. Girls played hopscotch or jumped double Dutch, and boys played catch or stickball.

Mothers, grandmothers, and aunts hung their heads out the windows to keep watch over the children. Every summer a screaming car braking too late would run over a boy running after a ball—it was always a boy—while a woman cried, pulled her head out of the window, slammed the door closed, and ran down the stairs to the damaged or lifeless body.

I don't know whether I was attracted to the children or the children were attracted to me. When I was first doing domestic work, I was involved with children. Not as deeply as most people, because I was actually not a babysitter; I was the housekeeper and the cook. They've always been fond of me.

There was a cousin, little Dennis, Cousin Dorothy's grandson, whom I really did take care of. He didn't get to go to the park unless I carried him to the park. His mother, his aunts, and his grandmother never did take him. The only place children can let out their extra energy is in the parks.

When I got married and Wendy was born, we would go to the park. I would always take something with us that two or three children could play with, because she was an only child. Because we were near the park, we would go down to what's now called Central Park North. We were on 112th Street between St. Nicholas and Lenox Avenues. We played in that park and we also played in Mount Morris Park up on the towers. That was a quiet park with a lot of swings and a playground, and there was a set of swings large enough for me.

Number one was that Wendy could not play in the street, because it was dangerous. But there were always kids up and down the street. We lived on the fourth floor. One child, Merry, who lived in the building, wanted

Wendy to come downstairs to play with her. I told her, "No, Wendy can't come downstairs."

I did not want to make the children feel that I did not want Wendy to be involved in their lives. So I asked Merry and her friends if they wanted to come up to the house. But they wanted to be out in the street.

I told them when we finished our work and came downstairs, they were welcome to come with us to the park if their parents said that they could. They were excited and happy about that. It was only on a Saturday if I wasn't working that we could go to the park.

We formed a group. We would go down to Central Park and play, then we'd come back home. Sometimes we might be able to get something to eat out in the street, but most of the time we came back home and I gave them all a treat. We did that until Wendy grew up and she was old enough to go to school.

She was in high school when we formed the club for taking them to Sunday school. Wendy took them to Sunday school, and I was a part of them. I was trying to see if I could help them to understand what education was about and how they had to study and not play so much in the street.

I decided to see if the parents would let me take them to her school. Wendy was in the dancing class and the drama class. The school would have recitals at night. The plays, for instance, would be presented at night. I wanted the children to be able to see what they could achieve if they studied. Maybe one of them could get a good education at Dalton or a school like that.

Actually, if they would read a lot, whether the schools were educating them or not, they could educate themselves. My goal was that my daughter would have exposure to the best of education, so that was why I worked on three and four jobs to send her to private school. I wanted the children of the neighborhood to be exposed to the same thing that Wendy was exposed to.

Sometimes there would be five or six of them. But we always had at least four children, all about the same age. Whoever wasn't busy or whenever their parents weren't doing something with them, I could keep them. The parents usually gave me permission to take them.

I was shocked by something one of the children said one day when I took them to Wendy's school. Pat, who had to be around nine or ten, wanted to go to the bathroom, so I told her where it was.

On our way home, she said to me, "Mrs. Jones, that bathroom was clean!"

"The bathroom was clean?"

"How do they keep it clean?"

"They have the custodians and the cleaning people who clean the bathroom, but the children have to help keep it clean, too. You can't spill anything without telling the custodian so he can wipe it up if you can't wipe it up. And you have to put your papers in the baskets where they belong. You help keep it clean."

"Oh."

"All bathrooms—your bathroom isn't clean?"

"No, the bathroom isn't clean. It's never clean."

"I can't believe that."

"Why don't you go see?"

I didn't go look at her bathroom at that time. This particular day we had been to the park. We stopped at my home to get some refreshment. So Pat goes into our bathroom. I think I was the first person to put a curtain around the bottom of the bathtub, because I couldn't stand the tub being exposed. I had made a frill to go around it. We had a real Victorian bathroom.

She came out of my bathroom saying, "Oh, Mrs. Jones, your bathroom is clean, too!"

"Honey, what is this about the bathrooms being clean? Don't you know bathrooms are supposed to be clean?"

"Well, I didn't know."

Because we stayed late that day, I walked the children up to their steps to make sure that the parents knew that they were home. She was living in a brownstone, which had the bathroom out in the hall.

I rang the mother's doorbell to let her know that I was bringing Pat home. The bathroom door was open, and I looked in. I understood what the child meant. The bathroom was filthy. Her school bathroom was filthy, too. Pat attended a New York City public school in the '60s.

I'd formed a club with the same group, trying to see if I could teach the young girls to cook. We were baking cookies. I know you have to start young with children. They started throwing the food around, so I had to stop that cooking class. I wanted to teach them the culinary arts, how to serve, how to become hostesses. But they had gotten too old. They were 10, 12, and 13 years old. It was too late for them, so I had to give that up.

Sometime near the end of 1996, the No Fear Gang was arrested by the police. A man named Lucas and his son were leaders of the gang. The two of them received sentences somewhere from 25 years to life. The gang had been making almost $3 million a year selling drugs.

I knew the father from when he was about seven years old. Lucas lived next door on the same floor. There again I thought I should be able to help people.

He was a wonderful young person. Lucas had a lot of talent. He was in the college-bound program for Columbia University, he ran track, and he played basketball. But it wasn't enough. Neither his family nor the community was there for him. The community that was there for him was only negative.

When Lucas and his sister Vivian were younger—Wendy went to Yale in '71—I took turns taking them up there so they could see the atmosphere of a university. I thought maybe I could get them interested in working hard, going to school. The young men up there talked to Lucas to see if they could keep him on the right track, but . . . we lost him.

After we came back from Yale, I called every social agency in the phone book, and went to Project Create, down there where Wendy met Butterfly McQueen. All the agencies said the same thing: they couldn't take him unless he'd been convicted of a crime, unless he was already a juvenile delinquent.

Lucas was a smart boy. Before I took him up to Yale, he and three of his male friends used to come up to the house. He asked me if they could play with Wendy's chess set. I told them to come on in. For about a month on Saturday and Sunday evenings he and his friends would come up to the house. Two would sit on the couch and two would sit on the chairs. I'd give them cake or soda, whatever I had around.

But the street was too strong. The drug dealers were recruiting them. And they got Lucas. The parent and the grandmother were not there for him. So I couldn't . . . I wasn't able to do it alone; the activities in the street, the money in drugs that he got involved in were far greater. And . . . we lost Lucas.

His sister, Vivian, was left behind in the fourth grade. She rang my doorbell and sat at my door. Wendy had gone away to college. She sat there, and worried me about getting left back. She wanted to be in the fifth grade.

"You'd go see about Wendy."

"Well, Wendy is mine. Yes, I'd go see about her. But your grandmother or your mother has to do it."

Every evening when I came in, Vivian would be at my door or she'd come over to my apartment to ask me to come help her.

So, finally I told her about what happened to me: "I got left back. It was me and my sister got left back, because we were out in the country. We didn't go to school for enough days. But it wasn't because we couldn't get our lessons. I wanted mother to go to school for me and tell the principal to let us try the fifth grade. We were in the same class that you are in. But my mother wouldn't go.

"So I went to school early one morning and asked the principal if we could go to the fifth grade, because we knew our lessons. He agreed, and we went on to fifth grade. Do you know the principal?"

"Yes."

"Do what I did. Go to school early one morning; tell the principal that you were left back. Tell her you could have gotten your lessons, but you just fooled around. But this time you will get your lessons and stay in class. Ask her can she get a tutorial program for you. I don't know if I can help you or not, but we should be able to get somebody at Columbia University to help you."

So she did. The principal granted Vivian's wish and told her she would put her on trial in the fifth grade. So Vivian went back and told her grandmother that she'd gotten into the right class.

Her grandmother came over to me and said, "Jonesie, I told you Vivian could take care of herself. Vivian went and told the principal. The principal said she could try the class."

"Mrs. Worthington, I want to underline it, parents were left here to take care of the children, not children to see about themselves. Vivian did not know how to go to that principal. I told Vivian what to do because I had been in the same situation that she was in, in my life. It worked for me fifty years ago, and it's working for Vivian now. If you ask, and ask in the right way, people will help you if they can."

"All right, Jonesie. Bye, I'll see you later."

She went home and she beat the child. And from that day on, Vivian didn't come by; she didn't say anything to me. But if she had let Vivian be a part of me, I believe I could have saved Vivian. It was too late for Lucas, but I could have saved Vivian. But she took Vivian away from me.

At 16, Vivian had herself a baby. As far as I know, she never did get married, but she just had that one child. But if the mother or her grandmother had been there for them, neither one of them would have ended up as they did, because they both were alert young people. This is my song: take care of the children while they're young and keep them in the greatest atmosphere.

I haven't lost the battle. I'm still working with children. Friday, when I was talking to someone, four little children from 121st Street saw me and they all came running to me. They wanted their hugs and their kisses. And they wanted me to see that they all looked very great in their little uniforms.

Children want somebody to let them know that they care about them, that they love them. This is what I find that the younger generation is not getting. Hopefully, we can work with the schools.

We have an elementary school across the street from us. I'm hoping that the new young people in the block can form a community group that can work with these young parents. The mothers and fathers are too young to be parents. They need the community, the church, the school to help with our young parents to see that their children get an early quality education. The public schools can't do it on their own.

I have too many nieces and nephews to count. There are approximately 35 or 40 nephews, nieces, great nieces, great nephews, great-great nephews, and great-great nieces.

I have been involved in their lives. I always went home for vacation during the summer, because my mother was there.

Every summer when I went home, I had a project for the children to do. I always carried a lot of paper with me so we could write. I would see who could sing and who could dance, which one could write and who could talk. We had something like a talent show. So I always had a lot of fun with them.

I knew that if they had somebody home they could talk to, we could get them interested in staying in school. Some of them get up, but they still don't want to go to school. I don't know whether they want to sleep late or what it is. Maybe the value of an education hasn't been taught. I would instill in them how important it is to create. You don't always have to go to college.

It's what's bothering me about the educational system. It is destroying all the children, not just the black children. They don't have anything to grow on. We have to find a way to give them the fertilizer that they need to grow, at the time that they need it. Start on them at birth, but make sure by the time that they are one year old that you are exposing them to the elements that they should have, a learning environment, and teaching them what their mind is for.

I have a feeling that most of the children don't even know what "mind" means. They don't know that they can develop it into what they want it to be, because there's nobody there to tell them. It doesn't just come from the parent. People don't seem to look at the environment that adults have created for the children.

All my great nieces and great nephews wanted their parents to do for them what I'd done for my daughter. Wendy used to go there every summer when she was little, until she was 12 years old. That was my goal for her, to learn about the family. And she did.

I guess Wendy was already determined that she was going to write. My mother was a great storyteller. The two of them read the Bible together, and my mother gave Wendy the family history. So she has been able to document that.

I was very grateful that Wendy was the one who did do it. She is in the first generation of grandchildren. Nobody in the family, of the great grands or the other children, spent the time with Big Ma that Wendy did.

They all wanted to know what they could do to be like her.

I told them: "You just have to be yourself. You can't be Wendy. Be the best that you can.

"Decide what you want to do and work hard at it. There are a lot of free things. The Y has activities, the library . . . you have to read a lot. One of the most important things in life is reading. You have to keep on reading and create what you want. You get visions."

My sister, Nora, didn't want to go to college. She didn't want any part of it. After she came to New York in

1963—Nora was just 28 years old—I tried to get her to go to college; she would not go.

I tried to get her to go to the bank, where she could have a career. But she wouldn't do anything but go back to the textile factory. I never saw anybody who would come all the way here from South Carolina to go back to the factory, to push another iron.

And those nieces and nephews of mine . . . Greenville Tech had some of the best technical courses in America. And nobody—*nobody* decided that they would go there to take any kind of courses or anything. Three of them finished high school, and that was the end of it. Nobody else ever finished high school.

There was talent in that family, but there wasn't anybody there to channel it. If one had made it out, maybe they would have survived.

CHAPTER 9

BUYING THE BROWNSTONE

My mother took a course at NYU called "How to Purchase a Brownstone" and bought a book entitled You Don't Have to Be Rich to Own a Brownstone, *by Paul and Joy Wilkes (Quadrangle/New York Times, 1973).*

After I graduated from Yale in 1975, Mama gave me her notes from the class and asked me to find a brownstone for us instead of getting a summer job. I was leaving for Tokyo in September on a two-year contract to teach English as a Second Language in a Japanese girls' high school.

Collecting my research in a notebook, I found the house before I left. Mrs. Thomas's daughter was showing the house for her mother, who lived in Long Island. Negotiations began. Then abruptly ended. In my notebook, Mama found a phone number with a

Long Island area code and no name. She called it on Thanksgiving Day.

"Mrs. Thomas, why did you take the house off the market?"

"Baby, it was taking so long. Didn't you have enough money?"

"I can afford it. I'm sorry. I had the wrong lawyer. I'll get a real estate lawyer, and everything will be ready in 90 days. "

"But I've already paid the taxes for this quarter."

"I'll reimburse you for the taxes on top of the purchase price."

"All right."

I closed on the house on March 1, 1976. I feel a warm connection to the house, because it was built during the period of time that my mother and my father were born. My father was born in 1886, the year of the earthquake in South Carolina. And my mother was born in February 1888, the year of the blizzard in New York City. This house was commissioned in 1884. The builders started work in 1885, and it was completed on January 1, 1887.

I am so enthused about this man's house, because I feel like he designed it for me. I would've told him to make it that way for me: the stained glass, the architectural woodwork in here. Now it's mine. I want it as a place where anybody that wants to can come in and see the work of the architect, Kimball. Then I can pass it on to Wendy.

CHAPTER 10

LOSING CREATIVITY AT WORK

In 1981, Standard Brands contracted with Office Canteen to take over the employees' cafeteria. Creative control of the cafeteria was now out of my mother's hands. Despite this, Mama kept as much control as she could over the cafeteria staff and the daily operations.

Her situation is similar to what happened in manufacturing in the United States in the 1970s, and what happened with customer service departments, computer programmers, and technical writers in the 1980s and 1990s as their work was outsourced to other states and other countries to cut costs. My mother's experience shows the effect of outsourcing on one creative individual.

From day one, things began to change after this new man came in. As far as I was concerned, I had no problems with Ross Johnson, CEO of Standard Brands, but he was not a man that was for the employees. He was there to get what he could for himself. I really didn't expect him to do anything for our department.

We were one of the departments that served all the people. I must say that in the thirty-one years that I handled it, the whole time that I, myself, was in charge of the food, there was never any food poisoning or anybody bringing food back and saying it was not right. You had to work hard with it; we always had a class A operation. All the purveyors that came through the cafeteria were amazed at what could be done with the limited equipment that we had.

I improved a lot of the equipment in the food service line. You take the coffeemaker . . . When I started working for Standard Brands, we used an urn. You had to pour five gallons of hot water over the coffee. You had to wait for about an hour for the electricity to get hot to heat the water in the morning before you could make it.

The salesman came in from Blickmann, the company that was the maker of that coffee urn. I was talking to him—this was in '53 when I first started with Standard Brands. I think I weighed 102 pounds soaking wet. I said, "This is very strenuous. You have to stand up on a stool to pour the water into the urn. Isn't there a way to invent something—like the garden sprayer—that you could spray the water over the coffee? Isn't there a way that this water could stay medium hot by using a thermostat where it could stay on low? Then you could come in and turn it up and it wouldn't take it any more than about fifteen minutes to boil. The way we have to do it now is too time-consuming."

He came back again and kept asking me what I wanted the engineers to do. I showed them. I wanted some arms up in there to spray the water over the coffee. We'd put the coffee into the basket and spray the water over it. In addition, I said, "It needs a mixer so it can churn it up and down just like we used to churn the milk—it turns it up and down so you don't have to repour it."

This was in '53. By '54 or '55, that urn was on the market, but I didn't get any credit for it. It was out there, that automatic, self-filling urn.

The people who are using things are the ones who can create inventions. The person who's out there selling doesn't know what you need. At least I got better working conditions. I didn't have to finish breaking my back to pour that water over the coffee. We got the self-filling urns in 1957 when we moved to 625 Madison Avenue.

When we were getting ready to redesign our cafeteria—this is before Mr. Weigl left; after that, it all went down the drain—two men were taking our coffee from floor to floor on a coffee cart. Wiley and Smythe—who designed the kitchen in the Windows on the World restaurant in the World Trade Center—designed our cafeteria.

He was sitting down talking to me about the layout. I said, "What's going to happen to the coffee?"

"I guess you're going to take it around like you have been—"

"No. We're moving into the eighties and will soon be in the nineties. We are not gonna take any coffee around anymore."

"What are we gonna do?"

"Take a walk with me. There's some space here that can be utilized. There should be a pantry on each floor where the coffee will be made. We should have a cabinet to keep the supplies in, and a refrigerator and a sink. We'll have a little tabletop stove, like a hot plate. People who want a cup of soup can heat it up."

As we walked outside the cafeteria I said, "On each floor there's a wing like this. I know there's an exit, but you don't have to close the exit. There's enough space, if you redesign this place. You can have the coffee urn on one side and the cabinets on the other. The person taking this coffee around just has to go to each station on each floor, put the coffee in, and go about his business.

He doesn't have to wait for it to finish. He's gone. We'll get twin urns. One is for hot water for tea and one is for coffee; two gallons is enough.

"That's my idea of a place functioning right. When the employees come in, they don't have to wait for you to bring the coffee around. The coffee is already made. You don't have to take the milk around every day, because you have refrigeration. Everything is there; the napkins, everything."

"You sold me. This is what we'll have."

He did not get to finish designing it. Another company picked up the construction part for Standard Brands. We finally did do the cafeteria.

But the new design kept those coffee pantries. I got calls from as far away as Chicago, from other Standard Brands offices. How were we dispensing our coffee? We were the first to have what I call a coffee pantry. Every new building that has gone up since then has that coffee pantry.

Credit never goes to the person who does the designing. You get some kind of reward for it, but you don't get money. I got the satisfaction of knowing that we did have a functional place where we didn't have to drag the coffee through the halls anymore. Before we made that change, folks had been getting burned. And there were spills and complaints about it wasn't hot. We didn't get any more complaints.

When Ross Johnson came in, the cafeteria was still being redesigned. I wasn't involved in it; in order to design a cafeteria, you have to have the menu.

When the kitchen man came in and was talking about the cafeteria layout, I said, "Whose menu are you going to work by?"

"We got the one from up in Connecticut."

"Who gave you our menu?"

"You'll use the same menu that—"

"Oh, no. That's a test kitchen. This is a cafeteria—an employees' cafeteria. If they're gonna be in charge of it, we'll work by their menu. But if it's going to be here in New York and I'm in charge of it, we'll have our own menu."

"I don't know . . . they just said—"

"Whoever you're talking to, you tell them that we will not work with menus from the test kitchen, because they are not cafeteria people. They don't know what these people eat. I know what they eat." Then I'd been with the company about 26 or 27 years.

He went back to whoever he was talking to, came back, and said, "Mrs. Jones, you make out the menu for a week, then you make out one for a month. This way I can design the equipment that you need and the kitchen."

So I gave him those menus and one for six months.

My boss came in and said to me, "How do you rate getting this?"

"I will not do anything from the test kitchen. I know what I need."

"All right then, do it whatever way you and the kitchen man decide."

The kitchen man said, "Mrs. Jones has been looking at blueprints. She knows exactly what she wants and where the things go. There's no need for you to tell me anything. Mrs. Jones knows what she's talking about."

The head of the test kitchen puts cabbage and ham on the menu on a Monday. You already had heavy meals over the weekend. You don't eat that kind of food on a Monday. Most every one of the employees who came through there, I knew their taste.

Then when they weren't asking me anything, I knew. . . They kept telling me... Rumors were flying... First, they were going to move it up on the eleventh floor. We were going to have an atrium there. Then they said they were going to have it down on the ninth floor. Next I heard we were going to go out on the roof.

Finally, I went and asked what was going on.

"You'll be in charge."

"But where are the menus?"

"It'll be set up in keeping with your ideas."

So I just went on and left them alone. But I knew something was going on. They'd asked me for the prices of everything. Why did they want my price list?

This is what they were doing: they were giving the food to an outside service. It was very painful, but I knew it was their job; it wasn't mine. And the employees were the ones who would have to suffer; I didn't have to eat the food.

I tried to tell them this was a food company. We should give our employees the best of food, nutritious food.

They said it would be so much cheaper and it would be this and it would be that and you would keep the job and all this. I said, "Yes, that's fine, but after all these years waiting for a cafeteria, for a functioning place, and then you decide to give it to somebody else. But that's your decision; it's not mine."

Then they were going to drag me around to sample the food from the outside service. It was all centralized. We went down to their headquarters, to the commissary, somewhere down on 14th Street, on the West Side to inspect the cafeteria. Because I didn't carry on about how good the food was, something was wrong with me. But it didn't matter. I'm in control of me. Maybe one thing they could do was fire me. That's the only thing they could do... So when management asked me how the food was, I told them what I thought.

"It's not my kind of food. It is a step below what I would buy anyplace. I don't serve this kind of food. But this is your company, your people. I'll serve your people what you give me to serve them."

So they left me alone. I kept going backwards and forth to see what they were doing. First they were going to give me a nice office, then they gave me this little cubbyhole. So then we had to fight about that.

All right, when they got it all built, this Mr. Farley had made out the menu. Four white guys and one black woman. One was my boss and the others belonged to Klein's company, Office Canteen. They were going to tell me what we were going to do.

This was the eighties; I was living in the brownstone. I walked down past 112th Street, where I used to live, to 110th Street. I had to review my life; I had to think about what I was going to do. This was a big step. This was going to be the day that I relinquished my responsibilities, something I worked hard for . . . I was thinking about the time I went back to school . . . I'd put an awful lot into it for them just to say, "You are nobody. We are going to bring somebody else in to take over the job. You've got to serve their food."

I had to figure out what I should say and do to protect myself and my staff.

The meeting was at ten o'clock. I got there and they were sitting around a round table talking about how gorgeous the cafeteria looked and what great food we were going to have on opening day.

This Mr. Farley looked at me and said, "We've made out the menu and we've decided that you would do the salads for that day."

I said, "Excuse me?" That's one way of giving yourself time to think. So he repeated himself.

"Well, Mr. Farley, I don't know if you know my background, but you're looking at a woman who went back to school at 42 to get the credentials that she needed to handle this job. I came out at the top of the class. I had a science award.

"I know what kind of food to serve in health and disease. I have been feeding these folks so they could be healthy, even had salt-free bread here. Anybody on a special diet only had to tell me what their diet consisted of, and their food was there for them."

One of the guys said, "There is no such thing as salt-free bread."

"That's because you don't know. I know there is salt-free bread. Nobody asked me anything when you were making out this menu. I know what these people like.

"It's your day. For twenty-eight years I have toiled here with these people. I've had my glory. I had a wonderful time. I enjoyed every moment of it. It's been hectic, it's been hard, it's been painful . . . and it's been joyful. But I'll tell you, the joy outweighed the pain because I was happy doing what I was doing.

"And I must say, the management I have had has been in back of me 100 percent. I have stacks of letters to prove the things that I have done and the people that I have served. I have it in writing, so I'm happy. Now Monday when we open up that cafeteria, it will be your day, not my day. You make the salads, not me. And another thing I want you to know.

"The way you bring that food in there—if it's to be kept cold, I'm going to keep it cold until it's time to serve it. If it's to be kept hot, I'm going to keep it hot until it's time to serve it. And I'm not putting anything in it. Because I would be furious if I sent out any kind of food and somebody else put something in it. That's your day. The job for me and my staff is merely to see that your food is set out there presentable. We will do that, but none of my extra work will go on it."

Nobody knew what to say or do. Until finally my boss spoke up and said, "Well, you know, Jo, you got a point there. It is your day. Why don't we just do it the way you want to do it?"

"Yes, anything suits you, suits me. This could have been done peacefully if you had consulted me. But you didn't. You left me out of the whole thing until you got it all fixed. Now it's too late.

"Don't nobody come in and tell me what to do. I'm going to always be my own boss."

"Fred is the manager over this."

"No, he isn't the manager over me. Whatever food I order, you send it."

"We make up our menus for the week."

"That's all right. I'll order whatever you got on the menu. I will not change it, because I do not have to eat it." I underlined it, "I do not have to eat it. You are feeding the people; you're not feeding me."

So they all got up and left.

Then when I introduced Fred to the staff, I told them the same thing: that we were merely here to set his food out. As far as the sanitation code was concerned, we had always gotten a good rating and we would still get one.

"As far as our art is concerned, it's over. It's over, it's just over." So, we didn't have too much trouble. But I always had to put them in their place.

Fred sat down and started telling me how to order and what to do and what not to do.

"If you got anything you want to tell me about your food, give it to me in black and white. Fred, while you were trying to get to the United States (he was from Yugoslavia), I had learned and forgotten what you are trying to learn. So don't come in here telling me to order something today, and tomorrow you order something else and you put the first things in last and the last things in first. My staff is already trained. There's nothing you can tell me."

"All right."

"Don't cross the line. If I want to know anything from you about this food, I will call and ask you. It's one of the things I will do, because I don't want to know.... It's yours, it's not ours."

"You'll taste it—"

"No, I don't taste anything. If food doesn't look to suit me, I don't taste it."

"How you gonna know—?"

"I didn't make it; you made it. I don't want to know. . . It's yours, it's not ours. Ours was finished when the cafeteria left the tenth floor."

We had a mixture of their staff and our staff working in the cafeteria. If it hadn't been for me being there as long as I had, they would have eliminated the whole crew, but they couldn't. I refused to allow them to let any of my people go.

All my people were there. I introduced all my staff and gave them what they were responsible for. "We will follow the instructions labeled on your pans. I've been to your commissary. It's not up to my standards, but you're not cooking it for me."

"We have first-class food, and everything is fresh."

"It's not nutritious, and I don't have to eat it."

So we didn't get into too many fights. I was not going to let him do me like they were doing those other managers that they had. God works in mysterious ways: They didn't have it a year before another company bought them out. And we weren't there two years before Nabisco had us. So it was over.

Food is for health and for beauty. It's one of the things that keeps us going, gives us happiness. I've been reading some books that date from the beginning of the 1700s on food. I found out a lot about the history of food preparation.

I think it was April 6, 1981, when the real Standard Brands cafeteria switched over to Office Canteen's Food Service. It was the last of April before we actually opened up on the eleventh floor, because they hadn't finished the cafeteria up there.

After that, when they came downstairs to the tenth floor, where the cafeteria was originally, Office Canteen's people wanted to take all our food and wedge it in with their food.

I said to them, "No, we're not going to do that."

"What are you going to do? Give it to the poor?"

"That's right. Standard Brands paid for it; they'll not pay for it twice. You're going to get it and resell it to us or sell it to somebody else. You're not taking my food from down here." (I was talking about the food that was in the refrigerators and the canned food that was in the storage room.)

They would never tell me exactly when they were going to close, so I wasn't able to judge what food we would need. They didn't let me know what day we were moving upstairs until it was too late for me to cancel some of the orders I had. So I just let it come on.

I gave it to the help and to the elevator folks and to Father Mike. He had a soup kitchen. So that was how we got rid of the excess food. The head of Office Canteen complained to Reston about it.

Reston said, "Well, Jo is in charge of that."

The first day we had the setup, they had fresh roast beef.

The employees of Standard Brands said, "Oh, look what we got. We didn't have this downstairs and we didn't have that. Look what we have now . . ."

I said, "Wait till tomorrow."

Johnson ate there occasionally, but he had eaten in the cafeteria more when we were on the tenth floor than he did when we moved to the eleventh floor. The first day they opened up, he got the roast beef. He and Mr. Gray came up. He was saying I was in control of the cafeteria, and look what a wonderful job I had done.

I told him too, "Wait till tomorrow. We are not in control of this, Mr. Johnson."

And tomorrow did come. The next day everything came in there frozen, precooked. You had nothing to do but put it in the convection oven and up on the steam table. Everything was already made. We got the tuna fish two or three times, and it was sour.

Finally, I said, "I refuse to serve it, and I'm not sending any more back. I've been in food for twenty-nine or thirty years, and I have never had a food poisoning complaint. I am not going to sit here and get one now. I will tell management downstairs I am not buying your tuna fish."

Fred said, "All right, Mrs. Jones."

"And don't send us any more chicken salad either. I'm not accepting any more of your ready-made salads, because they are not up to the Board of Health standards, and I know it."

I would order our own tuna, in the can. We made and mixed our own tuna salad.

Maybe a couple of weeks after opening day, Mr. Johnson ordered a roast beef sandwich. They sent the roast beef out precooked and frozen. We thawed it out and made a sandwich out of it; I sent it down.

We took what fat we could get off it. We couldn't get all the fat off it because there was fat all over.

Johnson told his secretary, Lisa Wells, to call me up. "Jo, Mr. Johnson does not like the roast beef that you served him today."

"Tell Mr. Johnson that makes two of us. Standard Brands is not in control and I'm not in control. I don't eat the food. This is what you get when somebody else is in control. This is what we were doing with the cafeteria when it first began. You took it and put it in the street, so you eat it. And I don't want to hear another word about it. Don't complain to me. Complain to Office Canteen and to Reston about it."

She said, "I didn't mean—"

"I'm just telling you now. I don't want to hear it. You can tell him what I said or you can keep it, but don't call me anymore."

She didn't call me anymore to complain about it. I don't know whether she complained to Reston about it or not.

All the meatloaf was nothing but fat. The Standard Brands employees started complaining to me that it didn't taste right.

"I told you I don't eat this food. I don't taste it."

"You don't taste it? Why—"

"If I had cooked it, I would taste it. I don't know what's in it. You people just find somebody else to complain to, and that's management. Don't complain to me."

Reston was the head of the cafeteria and my supervisor. He and his group couldn't control it because they didn't know anything about food. But they felt if they could get it out of my hands, they would be able to control these other people.

What they didn't understand was if you don't know anything about food, you can't control anybody. This was why I created the cafeteria for Standard Brands, so we could know what we were eating.

Before, whatever we bought that wasn't right, I could send it back to the purveyors. This man was telling us he made it yesterday and it's been cooked ten or fifteen days before.

If I asked for anything that was in the market, and it wasn't top quality, the vendors I'd had before this outside service came in, would tell me, "Mrs. Jones, we have it, but it's not for you." And they didn't send it.

With these new people, everything was grade B. You didn't have grade A anything, including eggs. The little eggs they sent were grade B eggs, but we were paying grade A prices for them. Standard Brands didn't know, but I knew.

I was going to see that the money was spent wisely and see that Standard Brands' employees had the quality of food that we needed. And that we had nutritious food.

I wouldn't have this roast beef with this much fat on it. Well, the people at the company wanted something different, so they got it.

Once they had a meeting with all of us, and Reston and his group said I was just picking on the food. I said, "If I am picking on their food, why does Johnson call me up and say that he didn't like the type of food being served? Why? That's not me. I don't complain about anything."

"We just don't want you to complain."

"You call Mr. Johnson. I didn't make that complaint. Here is a piece of the meat that you can smell. This meat came in like this. Now where has it been? I don't know. How many days has it been cooked? I don't know."

"It must have gotten mixed up with somebody else's meat."

"It shouldn't be down in your commissary. It should have been in the garbage in the first place. It shouldn't be there to be sent out to anybody."

Reston said, "I didn't think that you would be so upset."

"I'm not upset about it. Just tell the people not to complain to me anymore. I can't control the food."

Well, it wasn't long . . . the head of Office Canteen was there about a year before Office Canteen was taken over by another company from Europe. But for a while they kept the plant down on 14th Street.

They had an office somewhere out in New Jersey, too. Mr. Farley carried me out to New Jersey to see their plant. They all were doing the same thing. Nobody was preparing nutritious food and nobody was using grade A products. Everybody was using grade B products, trying to get as much profit as they could and spend as little as they could.

We had that food throughout '82 and '83. A lot of people started gaining weight and having high blood pressure. They complained to me about it.

"I do not want to hear it. You cannot eat this kind of food and not get some kind of ailment if you eat it on a daily basis. Most of you are eating it as your main meal of the day, and you're eating the wrong food."

Whenever the whites are in control of something, it is right, but if there is a minority person in control of it, it could be done a different way. Even if it could be better, they don't say anything about it when it's not good.

It didn't get me down. One of the things I had to look back on was that I had done wonderful things with food.

I just decided I would collect my salary and move on to other things. I would have been able to move into a new position if I had known exactly when they were closing the old cafeteria. If I had found out in '76 when Mr. Weigl left that it was closing, I think I would have gotten out then. I would have gotten into a position in food where I would have been recognized for my creativity.

It was painful at times. In fact, years before I was ever recognized as much as I was in food, some of the employees said I was wasting my time there. Although the employees appreciated the food, the company didn't appreciate my knowledge and the energy that went into creating it.

CHAPTER 11

THIS PARTY'S OVER

Acquired Immune Deficiency Syndrome (AIDS), for decades a chronic disease requiring those with the infection to take as many as 25 pills a day, seems to have a cure in sight. In 2008, the first person, a man known as "the Berlin patient," was cleared of the AIDS infection via a bone marrow transplant and gene therapy. By 2011 there were upwards of 1.1 million people in the United States living with the disease, and 33 million worldwide, most in developing countries. The glimmer of hope for a cure was welcome news; however, the early years of the AIDS pandemic, which was first seen in North America in 1981, rivaled those of the beginning of the black plague.

Although most people now feel they know everything there is to know about this disease transmitted through bodily fluids such as sperm, blood, and saliva, what is often forgotten is the hysteria this disease brought with it in every community in which it was discovered. Couple this with the shame accompanying any disease which can be sexually transmitted and you have an emotional firestorm. It didn't help that in a homophobic society it was first found in gay men. Discomfort with discussing how AIDS was contracted led, in 1983, to the widely publicized erroneous information—reported by National Institutes of Health's Dr. Anthony Fauci— that people could be infected with AIDS through casual contact, such as sharing the same living space.

Police officers demanded elaborate body and hand coverings when dealing with people suspected of having AIDS; nurses and doctors refused to treat AIDS patients, and children with AIDS were banned from schools. And the Band Played On *by Randy Shilts details this atmosphere of terror.*

My cousin, Ken, was a professional butcher addicted to heroin. By November of 1984, when he entered the hospital, the number of AIDS patients in the United States totaled 7,000.

I don't say I retired; they just kicked us out. We didn't get to retire, and that was the thing that hurt most. Because we were a service group, there wasn't a ceremony. Every other group that retired from there had had a ceremony, which was the end of the journey.

My last day at Standard Brands was November 30, 1984. The precursor of that was that we had to sign a release that we were satisfied with what they were giving us as severance pay, one week for each year. All the other groups that left there, except us, the service group, got two weeks' pay for each year that they had been there. I had been there 31 years, so I came up with just about eight months of severance pay. It was . . . a letdown.

I didn't sign my release. Everybody else in my group signed. First place, I did not sign because I did not belong to the company that they had signing us off, which was Lifesavers. I'd worked for Standard Brands; we became Nabisco Brands when they merged. After Standard Brands' former people found out I wasn't going to sign, they sent their man, Mr. Langley from human resources, over to talk to me.

"All right, Jo. We won't push you to sign. We'll let you make that decision when you get ready. We'll be in touch."

"Ironically, you've come to me on November the 30th. I've had to make a lot of decisions on this date in my life. They've all been painful. My husband deserted the baby and me thirty years ago this day. You come to me to sign away the 31 years of my life that I've worked. No, I can't sign it."

"We won't press you." He said, "I didn't know you were having a party, Jo. I would have stayed for lunch."

"You should have known, Mr. Langley, that I was not going to leave here on a sour note. I didn't have a thing to do but tell Mr. Klein that we wanted a party. I don't care whether it gets paid for or not. I was going to leave here on an up beat."

"You sure are leaving on one." He took the paper and left.

I had my feelings written on the cake: "This party is over." I never did feel like I was going to work. I hope everybody that worked in the environment that I worked in felt that way, too.

I could buy what we needed. And I could use it the way that I wanted to use it. Had I not had that job, I would not have had the opportunity to develop into the culinary artist that I developed into.

Ken, my nephew, Vera's son, had been coming around, and I could see that he was sick. But I didn't know what was wrong with him. My nephews, my brother Calvin, and my sister Sally's friend came down on the

30th in Sally's car to pick me up to bring my things back from the cafeteria.

Wendy had come down for that day because she had been a part of that job, too. She had been coming to visit on that job since she was one year old. Wendy had made a lot of warm and caring friends in that company. I guess that was one of the things that made it feel so special to me, too—that Wendy had been special to that company. I don't think anybody ever worked in any company that had the contact that I had had with the president of the company.

It came from me feeding the people and making sure that their food was up to health standards and was exceptional. We always got handwritten notes from Mr. Weigl (he became head of the company in 1964). I was introduced to whoever came to that company. They were told about Wendy and they were told about how I took care of her. That made life much easier.

If I had had the problems on the job that I had with other elements in my life, I couldn't have survived. I always knew that when I went to work there was some pleasantry there, something that I could find that would take away the pain. That's how I became creative, taking away the pain.

I had made contact with Carol Brock and the *New York Daily News* and the head of research and development at the News. They all had told me anything that I wanted to do or wanted to get involved in to just let them know and they would be there for me.

After my family came here that Friday, it took Ken so long to get anything done; I said to my brother, "Calvin, he's sick."

"I don't know, Jo. He just lies around all the time. He always did lie around. But it looks like to me he's even slower now. I think he is sick."

Anyway, Ken went up to Sally's house. That was Friday night. On Saturday morning sometime, December 1, he ended up in Columbia Presbyterian Hospital. From then on, my life, my days, my hours were not the same anymore. He was 38 years old.

That was my time, and I got pushed over into that. Everybody was working but me. I did feel like being an aunt to him—even though this family had leeched on me all the time—I had to be there for him.

If I hadn't had connections with the administrative part of Columbia Presbyterian, he would have died in the next couple of weeks. I don't know whether we were right in keeping him alive that long or not, but God had a hand in it. I was able to get the pastor of our church to intercede with the administrators at Columbia Presbyterian Hospital so that he received excellent care.

We had excellent contact with the doctors. The top doctors would come and talk to us. They told us that they were doing more for him than they had done for others with AIDS.

The three months Ken was there, I went to the hospital sometimes twice a day, but always at least once a day. I was there with my sisters Nora and Sally, and Vera, his mother. Nina, Vera's daughter, wasn't there.

I told the doctor he was sitting among a group of women who had over a hundred years of working in public service in New York. We came from a strong black family in the South and had a great mother and a great father. The lifestyle that our nephew had chosen for himself was not part of a family situation. Vera didn't say anything.

"It comes from the atmosphere of the time that we're living in, that causes him to be here in this condition. I want you to know that you are looking at a mother who has lost two sons to this atmosphere. She lost a son in '77 who was 24 years old to drugs. As far as we know, this AIDS is because of drug use. So we're devastated."

You could see the change in their faces. They all had a feeling for us as they got up and shook our hands.

One doctor said, "I thought one of the young men that came in here was him one day."

"That's Ben, his twin."

"I had to do a double take. How is he?"

"She has two sons out there, and they're on shaky ground. The niece we can say is fair, but the sons are on shaky ground. If something isn't done, we're going to lose them, too."

"I'm going to promise you one thing, Mrs. Jones. I'm going to get Ken back home."

"You put him back there, and God will do the rest for us. That's all we ask."

"Nobody has gotten the treatment that he's gotten here. We've tried every drug that we have."

We could go in at any hour. Vera stayed up there every night with him.

When Ken was ready to come home, there was a battle. He came home in early March of '85. I'd gone up to the hospital that day, but I didn't see the doctor until the next morning.

He said to me, "Mrs. Jones, what are your plans for Ken going home? We told his mother last night that he was ready to go home. I want you to know that we're on

24-hour call for you. If you want us to, we'll send a nurse home with him."

"His mother didn't say anything to me about it. She must not have understood you; she has a hearing problem."

"She understood me very well, Mrs. Jones."

"Vera has gone to work. But I'll talk to her. As you know, he does not have a home of his own to go to."

The next day, the hospital set up a meeting with the social worker. The social worker had to find out where Ken was going. Nora, my youngest sister, didn't go to that meeting. It was just me, Sally, and Vera.

The social worker said, "Ken is being discharged tomorrow. What are we going to do with him?"

Sally started crying. I knew it was bad then, because she doesn't cry; she curses. Sally said she couldn't take him home. She was the one that put him in the hospital. He left from her house. However, she couldn't take him home with her because her friend, Eddie, was sick. Sally and Eddie had lived together for many years. He died shortly after this time. Vera's other two sons were staying in their apartment, too, so she didn't have any space for Ken.

The social worker told us that the only alternative they had for Ken was to put him in Goldwater Memorial Hospital on Roosevelt Island.

"But we put too much in him for him to go to Goldwater. They're just going to put him on the side and nobody is going to feed him. He'll be dead in a couple of days. We don't want that to happen."

So . . . all right, she gets to Vera. "Mrs. Gorman, what are your plans for your son?"

"I can't take him. You have to send him to Goldwater, because I don't have any place for him."

"The only thing we need is a room. We'll give 24-hour service. We'll supply food. We don't want him to go to Goldwater. We want to see what this medication is going to do for him. We'll send an ambulance for him to come back to the hospital if he can't come back when it comes time for his return visits."

Vera said she couldn't take him. She was working.

"We'll give you 24-hour service. We'll take care of him."

Finally she came up with, "You know he has a stepfather. Things aren't too good there for him. So . . . no, he can't come to my house." She made no exceptions, nothing.

So then when the social worker came to me, I looked at her and said, "Well, we're not getting anyplace. Vera, you know, I've been with you through all your problems. Wendy has rebelled against me taking Ken, because she feels that if you are alive, you should take him, and she is right. He is yours.

"But I sit here today in between two things. I really can't see Mama's and Daddy's blood being treated like this. I can't see him going to Goldwater. I'm like the doctors. I've come here every day, every day. And I can't travel over to Goldwater every day.

"I'm going to have to go against Wendy. I'm going to fix a place there to take him home with me and let God do the rest." Most people at that time were afraid of AIDS, but I knew God would take care of me.

Vera lit up like a Christmas tree.

Nina, Vera's daughter, wanted to take Vera home that night. I told her I was afraid to stay there at the hospital at night by myself with Ken. So Nina left Vera alone. Then Nina had no interest in him. Nina and Vera got interested in him when they knew that I was getting his disability started for him.

I should have never let Vera come in the house after I brought him here. I should have just told her not to come help take care of him. I should have taken the nurses. Then I wouldn't have had to be in the situation of having all her children and grandchildren running in and out. But anyway, I didn't make that decision.

My mother brought Ken home and set up a bedroom in the front parlor on the couch that Big Pa had bought in 1939; she had reupholstered it in dusty rose. She put gold-flocked paper over the peeling plaster walls. Mama bought a white mug with Ken's name on it in black Gothic letters for him.

The couch was alongside the wall in front of the bay window with the stained glass. In the morning, the sun shone on his skeletal copper face in multicolors of red and blue and gold. Wrapped in blankets and a maroon afghan, Ken seemed more blankets than body. The room's fourteen-foot ceiling made him look even smaller.

Mama had found out from the hospital what precautions to take. She wiped down the toilet with bleach and washed his dishes separately. Every morning as I came down the stairs from my attic bedroom, I could hear my mother on the kitchen phone pleading with agency after agency, trying to get Ken's disability started.

After Mama brought Ken home, every evening her nieces and nephews swarmed into the house, bringing their barbecued potato chips and sodas with them.

In the meantime, we had a nurse coming three days a week. She was kind of like a psychologist; she talked to him and checked up on him. But I didn't ask any other nurses to come to the house every day. It was just cooking and feeding him. I could do that.

This is where I felt like I did wrong, because you had to cook for all of them. If I had left all of them out of the picture, then it wouldn't have been hard, you know. I just would have been cooking for him and taking care of him. All these things I didn't see.

If Nina didn't come for him, we'd get a cab and take him to the hospital. Most of the time Nina never stayed until we finished because she had to go to work.

The two of us would come on back home. We always got a taxi back. Most of the time Columbia Presbyterian gave us taxi fare, too. They reached all out. We got medicine. We got everything.

All right. Things were going pretty well and I was trying to assemble some veterans with disabilities to come in to talk to him, to tell him how they had come through. Of course, they had told us it was a death sentence.

Then all of a sudden, here came Nina into the picture. She wanted to take him down there to the Gay Men's Health Crisis Center; it had just started. But he was not gay. He was a drug user. And he did not want to go.

I still don't know if he got it from drugs or he got it from his girlfriend. His girlfriend had died in '81, and it wasn't diagnosed as AIDS, but she died looking just like he was looking. She was a drug user, too. We couldn't exhume the body to find out because they weren't married. AIDS had not been seen that much, especially among the heterosexuals, until the mid-1980s when he got it.

I didn't want Nina to take Ken to the crisis center, but she said her mother was in charge of him.

I gave them an ultimatum. "Take him and then take him on home with you. That's it. If you're going to be in charge of his activities or what we do to try to get him involved in not thinking about his illness, you do it all." I really don't think they thought I was going to do it.

I don't know why Ken didn't have sense enough to say something for himself, but I think they all thought that I was going to back down. I had made up my mind. "You wouldn't take him when you should have taken him, but now you're going to have to take him. You can't put him out here in the street."

They came and they got him. Vera said, "You know, Nina's going to do what she wants to do."

Nina was going to tell me all about myself and what I didn't do and what I had done. Her mother still wasn't saying anything. I couldn't understand Vera as a mother. Wendy had said something to Vera, and I told her to shut up because it wasn't her business. So Wendy went on away.

But Vera didn't say anything to Nina. She let her rant. Nina got her mother's silverware and her mixer. If I hadn't borrowed them and kept them, they would have been gone. Nelson, Nina's twin brother, who died of a drug overdose, used to steal everything in his mother's house to buy drugs. I had done so much for Vera that if I had kept my money, I could have bought silverware and a mixer.

I gave her money to pay on her children's car, when they had it, to keep her salary from being garnished. I never got my money back. These are the things that they always pull from you: See how much more I can take, how much more I can get.

Finally, Nina was going to tell me what my oldest sister had said. I told her, "If you plan to be a lawyer, you don't give out any information when nobody has asked you for it. If my sister wants to tell me anything, she knows my phone number, so I don't want to hear anything you have to say."

Nina still wasn't satisfied. She said that I wouldn't let her mother take her son, that I'd always been ruling her mother.

"Your mother never made any decisions. Vera, tell Nina what went on up there in that room that day. Tell her why I have your son. Tell her."

"Well, I didn't think it was going to turn out like it did." Vera thought he would've been dead sooner. That was what she meant.

Vera never did tell Nina the truth about it. I was not the cause of her not taking her son home. Nina said that Vera wanted to take him and I wouldn't let her take him. Her ma herself didn't want him. And she put it on her husband.

If it had been my son and my house, my child would have gone in there. Regardless of who was the father and who wasn't. If I had worked on two jobs like she had worked, I would've taken my son to my home. We would've gone home together or none of us would have stayed there in that house. But they took Ken.

Wendy: The night before Ken died, my cousin came to me in a dream: "Tell Aunt Jo I'll be leaving tomorrow."

He died on May 28, 1985, earlier than he would've died, but that was her child. I don't have any regrets.

Wendy: By the end of 1986, the year after Ken died, there were, according to the American Foundation for AIDS Research's website, 28,712 AIDS cases in the United States and 24,559 deaths.

That part of life has been very bitter. It's been very hurtful. I brought friction between me and my child. Then in the end . . . I was the villain.

It looked like Vera had never told Nina the truth about things. I was never the cause of her problems. If she had said she wanted her son, he would have been there with her. But I would have still been there to help her. Sally and Nora would have helped her. We wouldn't have left her alone.

I guess that's why Nina is so bitter with me now, but those are not my children. Those are Vera's children. I've done an awful lot for them, but I have one child, and that's Wendy.

I never had time to mourn the separation from the company. I got swept up in this. Then my thoughts and everything I was supposed to do . . . all my connections were gone.

I had the plan already *fixed* of what I was going to do. I had three or four invitations to go to Florida, down there to the retirees. I was going to go away for two weeks, then I was coming back.

I could have taken that kitchen in the brownstone and gotten started. I could have built up the business, then stopped and renovated. The purveyors were all there.

A year later, I didn't have that. People had moved on. Nobody had time to look back and say, "Can I help you?"

I feel like I've been blessed. They're still crying. I don't have any more of me to give anymore. What pennies I have, they're not going to get them.

When Wendy's father and I separated, I knew then that I had to take care of her. And I had to see about me. I had to stop giving, of my money and especially of my time. If I hadn't had Wendy, I would've been drained all my life. I never would've gone back to school. I never would've got the job at Standard Brands. I would've just stayed in domestic work so I could keep a job, so I'd be able to function, and let these people have what I had.

My daughter was the one I was working for, so that she could see that things could be done. When I came into the house and I was tired, my tiredness left when she greeted me. I didn't have any regrets about working three or four jobs for her.

When Wendy was 12 years old, she wrote me a letter saying that she knew the things that I could have done, the places that I could have gone if it had not been for her. But there wasn't any place that I wanted to go or anything that I wanted to do that Wendy kept me from doing, because I could take her with me. She wrote that she planned to make me proud of her.

I was supposed to go to Miss Dunfield's birthday party. She was my former supervisor at Standard Brands. It was the same date that Ken died. I was supposed to make a fruit arrangement to take to the party, because we were getting her a surprise party in a neighbor's house down there. But I couldn't go. My sister, Maude, offered to help me do the food, but I just didn't feel like doing it.

Miss Dunfield had closed everybody, including me, off from her. You could only talk to her on the telephone. She would not let you inside of her apartment. Then she fell. So she had to call one of the neighbors to come get her out of the bathtub. They took her to the hospital.

Then they understood why she wouldn't let anybody in the apartment. She and her sister, who was dead by this time, seemed to be pack rats.

Miss Dunfield was a woman from Lancaster, Pennsylvania. Her family brought the treasures from the home there, but there wasn't enough space for them.

Some of it must have rubbed off on me, because I have a whole lot of their junk here. It looks like I'm the pack rat now. I have to dig myself out of it.

Her beds were full; the couches were full. She slept on a chaise longue because she had junked up everything. When the neighbors were taking her to the hospital, she gave one of the people in the building the key to her apartment and my phone number.

She was in Lenox Hill Hospital. I went to see her before I went to the house. Miss Dunfield told me she wanted me to go there and see about her house for her. I can still see her. She had beautiful gray hair and a round face. When I walked into the hospital, she just reached up with both arms and brought me into her. "So glad to see somebody that loves you and somebody with some warmth."

She didn't have a family. She treated me like family. It was a warm feeling for me, too. It was my hug that she wanted. I told her she was going to get well. She would get back home and I would see about her. That was on a Sunday.

Monday I went down to the house. I opened the door; I could hardly get in. I'm small, but I had to turn sideways to get in, because the hallway was full of all kinds of debris. She and her sister just stacked chairs on top of chairs and tables on top of tables. Some of the things were very good things and some of the things were picked up in the street.

That was June. From June until September—Labor Day—I worked in there frantically, five days a week and sometimes six days a week. I was able to take out the good things and eliminate the bad things. Some of her good things I had to put in storage. Now I had space to work so I could get her back into her apartment.

When Miss Dunfield came out of the hospital, she went to stay with one of the neighbors on the same floor while I got the house cleaned up. I did a magnificent job. My brother, Calvin, came down and helped me. One or two of the ladies in the building helped. It was really a tremendous job. But we got it all cleaned out. The Saturday before Labor Day 1986, the neighbors made a potluck dinner and we welcomed her back into her apartment.

She died November 30, 1988, the same year Wendy got married. I told her that I was going to try to get Wendy and her life partner by to see her. But Miss Dunfield didn't get to see them.

Miss Dunfield was my dear friend, and I miss her because she was a person who I could talk to about all my problems.

EVERYTHING ELSE

15. FINISHING WATERMELON BOAT AT COMMUNITY EVENT

**16. SHOWING CULINARY ART TO TOYO EIWA
JOGAKUIN STUDENTS IN 1977**

17. FRUIT BOWL IN ESSENCE

18. ATTENDING MY YALE GRADUATION

19. HARLEM SONG CLIPPING

20. IN THE BACK PARLOR IN THE BROWNSTONE — HARLEM LOST AND FOUND

21. HARLEM LOST AND FOUND AT MUSEUM OF THE CITY OF NEW YORK

22. TURNING ONIONS INTO ROSES

23. THE CAKE: THIS PARTY'S OVER

24. THIS PARTY'S OVER

25. TRYING TO SIT WITH GRANDSON

26. ENJOYING PARIS

CHAPTER 12

COMMUNITY WORK

Before moving to the brownstone, Mama had organized a tenants' association at the apartment we lived in at 112th Street. The tenants put their rent in escrow and took care of the building. The goal was for the tenants to own and manage the building themselves. Everything fell apart when one tenant convinced the others that building ownership was impossible.

Mama now had a second chance. She intended to organize the homeowners on 122nd Street to take the community back from the garbage and the drugs.

In 1976, the drug problem was overflowing on 122nd Street between Seventh and Lenox where we lived.

After Wendy and I decided that this was the house that I could handle, I would come in the afternoon and watch to see if people were coming from work or whether there were people hanging in the street all day. I estimated that a lot of people who lived in the area were working people. The people that I saw every evening when I stopped by were actually people who didn't live in the block.

After I bought the house, I immediately looked around to see if we had a block association. I rang doorbells, but I could never find homeowners who were interested in working in the community. They said there had been a homeowner's association 35, or 40 or 50 years ago. I said, "What are we going to do? Are we going to let it go? I just bought my house and we have to restore it. We have to do a lot of work. The communities have to do it, because the policemen can't do it all." They didn't listen to me.

At least six buildings below me were vacant going toward Seventh Avenue. When I got off the bus on Seventh Avenue, I had to pass through all this blight, the drug dealers, the users, and the debris. You could smell it; I had to hold my nose because all the courtyards and vacant lots were full of everything. People would come from New Jersey and everyplace and dump everything in there.

I wondered how I was going to get it clean. I kept searching around. You couldn't find any answers, because nobody seemed to know an agency or anybody who was in charge. I asked a policeman, but he didn't know how I could get it clean. But first, I cleaned up the backyard of my house.

It took me two months to get it cleaned up. Dead cats and bones were back there. The people threw their garbage out of the window. Old dead trees, old pieces of wood . . . anything that they couldn't eat or wear was back there.

The garbage men told me that if I packed it up neatly, they would pick it up for me. Every evening when I came from work, I would work on the backyard. Then I had to work on the front.

In all these vacant houses, the front courts were just as bad as my back court was. A lot of it was construction debris. If people were working on a home and they didn't want to get a dumpster, they'd just bring it there in the middle of the night and throw it in the courtyards. All those vacant homes down there had been lost to the city for nonpayment of taxes. All had been owned by young black people. The parents had passed away and the young people would not pay the taxes. Almost all the houses from 143 all the way back toward Seventh Avenue were vacant. There were only two, 147 and 157, that were inhabited.

People would throw garbage in the court where you lived if they didn't see you out there. That's why you had to keep your court clean in the front, too.

I looked in the telephone directory and found our sanitation district. I called and spoke to the superintendent.

"How do we get the debris out? I can clean out my back, but I can't clean out all the others."

"Well, we don't expect you to, but we don't have any means or any money to clean it. But one thing we can do, if you get it up on the sidewalk, I'll send a truck to pick it up. It will be on a Saturday. We'll pick it up, but we have to have some of your men to throw it in, because our men can't handle it; it's not taxable garbage." He meant that no real estate tax was being paid on those buildings. The union didn't allow them to do it.

I bonded with some people in the neighborhood when I moved in. I named them the tree people. I bought the house the first of March, and by the time spring came, it was getting warm. And they would sit up there under the tree. The number of the house they used to sit in front of was 147. The tree was in front of 149, but 147 had people in it, so they sat up on that side; the shade was all over there.

Only three trees were in this block when I bought this house. There had been a tree in every space there was supposed to be, but people had killed them all.

I passed by Charles one day and said to him, "Charles, I want you to do something for me."

"What is it, Mrs. Jones? What is it you want?"

"I cannot stand this debris here. It makes me sick. I hold my nose and I go home and I still have that odor in my system. I don't know how you sit out here with it."

"I don't smell it, Mrs. Jones. I've smelled it so much, I don't smell it."

"If I paid you, would you get some of the guys to help you to take this up? The sanitation man said if I get this up on the sidewalk and you throw it in the truck, they will send the truck out here on a Saturday to pick it up. We have to make the arrangements a week ahead."

"All right, Mrs. Jones. When do you want us to do it?"

"I'd like you to do it next Saturday."

"I promise you, I'll get somebody."

"I'll get heavy-duty bags. You need boxes too, because some of this stuff won't go in the bags."

"Mrs. Jones, I'll get the boxes."

There were a couple of liquor stores in this area then. Charles started gathering up the boxes. I brought the bags. They must have been all week bagging it up. They put it up Saturday morning.

And we swept all the sidewalks on both sides. The school nearby was worse, except it was all up and down the sidewalk. We cleaned up the whole block. I did not, and I underline it, get a homeowner to help me. I paid the money myself. I made sandwiches for all the men who helped.

One forty-nine became vacant after I came here. The squatters burned it out. One homeowner's mother died and left him three houses in this block. They were fully paid for and fully rented when she died. He was an alcoholic. He would not pay the taxes, so the city eventually took the houses. They took the one that he was in, too. It must have been the '80s when the city took over his building. They started repairing it. The original doors had been destroyed. The city replaced the two wooden and glass doors with one cheap gray door with cement around it. He sat out there and drank wine. He didn't help clean up.

I paid them the first time to do it. The fall of 1976 was the first cleanup that we did. The next time, I started looking sad because we had to clean up again. People would come in the middle of the night when everyone had gone to bed. The tree people would not let them throw garbage in the courtyards in the middle of the day.

These were people in trucks. Sometimes guys would take a hand truck and go to other streets to bring stuff and throw it here. The people were paying them because they didn't want to hire a dumpster. That was how Harlem became littered. It might have been people from the Upper East Side. People would dump garbage wherever there were vacant buildings or vacant lots, and there was nobody there to protect it. I picked up magazines from Long Island and New Jersey out of the debris.

The next time, I still paid them to do it. But it didn't cost as much because we didn't let as much get in there. It was still 1976.

Then Charles, Mr. Teasdale, Mr. Lemming, and the others said to me, "Mrs. Jones, it's getting dirty again. It's not right that you pay us to clean it up. We all live here.

"No homeowner has ever cared anything about this block. But you came in here, and you want to revive it. We are going to help you. From now on out, we'll let you know when we're ready to clean it up and you just call a truck for us."

So I hugged them and kissed them and thanked them all.

I came from a clean family. Our area was clean—112th Street where we used to live—it wasn't half as bad as this. We scrubbed our own building down. The super wasn't there. I formed that tenants' group.

"I appreciate all your help, and it will be remembered. I'll tell it wherever I go. We are doing it. It's not the homeowners' community; it's our community."

And the Dogier brothers also helped keep it clean. One of the Dogier brothers didn't even live in the block. I think he lived on 120th Street. His brothers lived in the block, so he was always here.

There was a vacant lot down the block near Seventh Avenue. They filled it full of everything. People had started knocking down buildings and just dumping into the hole. It was much worse than the private courts; it was up over your head. Cars . . . everything was in it. We weren't able to clean that out because we needed dumpsters to put the debris in. The garbage people couldn't get that.

The vacant lot was different from the private ones, right near the corner. I don't know how many meetings I went to before I could find out who was in charge of it. This is all after I retired in '84. Those blocks had been vacant ever since I bought the house in 1976. I really didn't have time before to go to all these meetings. I went downtown to the Board of Health meeting about these lots. It came under sanitation, but not under our district. I found Commissioner Randy Dupree, who was assistant commissioner of environmental affairs. I went to him after the meeting and told him what was going on. He said, "Call me tomorrow and I'll give you a telephone number."

When it all comes down, the Pest Control people clean up. I called Miss Hilton one day and the next day she came out here; she walked through this area with me. Ms. Hilton told me, "Yes, I'll get it cleaned up for you, Mrs. Jones."

She sent the lot people to clean it up. It must have been about two or three days. This was '94. I'd been working on that a long time. I had the block cleanup in the spring and in the fall; I was the first person in this area to do this. Nobody knew what I was talking about when I said we were going to get the sanitation men to pick up the debris and we were going to sweep up the streets.

That is why I'd had such a poor relationship with the community, because nobody wanted to do the right thing. We could not survive in a neighborhood that was overflowing with garbage because people didn't want to follow the rules and regulations; some people do not adhere to the law unless it is enforced. That is what set me apart in the neighborhood; I wanted the right thing done, so there was something wrong with me.

I had my satisfaction; I know what I did. I know this is my work out here in this block with the other people here. It was my people in the block who cared about the block. We had one or two women, but most of them were men.

The other time a homeowner helped was in '85 when Ken died. We planned to clean it, and I got Miss Hawthorne to go out there with me. That was the only time there was a homeowner out there besides me.

The head of the community organization in the block was annoyed at me because I wouldn't give her my resources or how I got things done.

Before the vacant lot was cleaned up, she asked if I needed any help. I told her that if she had some youth to help her put out the flyers for the block cleanup, it was all right with me.

So she sent the flyers out, but she said that her organization was hosting it. I went back and told her, "No, this is not your project; this is my project." The block association had been doing this for years, and my name was not on there. I was like Ida B. Wells. She was angry when she was left off the list of the NAACP founders, and I was angry that my name was not on the flyers.

So Miss Hawthorne went back and put out some more flyers with my name and phone number at the bottom. But I didn't realize that she was doing this so she could get credit for it and not the block association.

I was still trying to get the teachers to park their cars in the back where they were supposed to park them. I always did two things at the same time. I would get the sanitation people to do one thing, and then I would call them about something else that was bothering me in the neighborhood.

I told the sanitation department that the teachers wouldn't move their cars so the street sweepers could clean the street and the custodians could sweep the sidewalks in front of the school. I had had to keep it clean ever since we had been here.

This was 1994. So the superintendent of our sanitation district said, "Mrs. Jones, I'll come up Monday and check it to see what is going on. I really don't know, because I haven't been involved in it."

When we were cleaning it, the head of the community organization wanted to go over on the school side and clean up so she could say what *she* was doing.

I said to her, "I'm sorry, but that is my evidence over there. The superintendent from the sanitation department is coming out Monday to check this. If we clean it, he is going to wonder am I crazy, what am I talking about? If I destroy the evidence, then I won't have a case. I've been working since December to get these teachers to move these cars. Do you see all that dirt, that dog mess and all that stuff up and down there? This is my opportunity; I can't let it go by."

She said, "I want it clean."

I looked right in her face and told her, "I'm sorry, this is not your project. This is the block association's project, and this has been going on ever since 1976. My evidence stays over there."

She walks up to me, puts her fist in my face, and says, "Woman, don't you dis me!"

I had never had anybody act like that toward me. I just walked away.

The problem is that in front of the school, they have certain rules for parking. I don't know what the distance is, but there isn't supposed to be any parking during school days within this area from 7 to 4. That's so the street sweepers can sweep the gutters. And the custodians were supposed to clean the sidewalk every day. We finally got a custodian who did that.

The superintendent looked up at the sign and said, "Mrs. Jones, you were right. No cars are supposed to be parked here between 7 and 4 on school days. You have a legitimate complaint. I don't know why they have allowed this to go on.

"In fact, on the back of the school where the teachers park, the custodians are supposed to be coming in at 7 o'clock in the morning to clean it before they get there. The street sweeper can't get there, because we gave them that parking space. No, this is wrong. We will make it right."

I don't know where I had been, but I came back early and the cars were gone. The cars were on the back where they were supposed to be between 121st Street and Adam Clayton Powell Boulevard. That is the teachers' space.

From then on, I didn't have any trouble with the garbage. Then they got concerned about the drugs. The tree people wanted to get the drugs out of the neighborhood.

"That's a legal battle. What I'll do now is go to the precinct and ask what help we can get." We went to the precinct and found out they were just sending out proposals for civilian patrols; I got an application.

"Mrs. Jones, you fill out the application and we'll work with you."

That's how the civilian patrols got started. It was mostly black men with walkie-talkies. We reported anything that was suspicious to the police, but we didn't carry guns. We did clean up the drugs in the community.

We started the civilian patrol with the block association. And the rest of the money was supposed to go to doing something within the block. So when anything happened, like the death of someone in the block, I would just take the stipend given to me for running the block association and give a donation. I would send flowers to the family. Laura was part of the school. A car hit her and a young kid got hurt with her, too. I went over to the school—that was my stipend—but I gave it to them from the block association to plant a tree.

Just this Easter past, I was on the terrace and this car drove up. He drove past the tree, got out of the car and went back there in front of the tree. I thought once he was going to go to the bathroom, because that's what they usually do, but he kept standing there with his head down and his arms folded. He stood there for about five minutes. I realized he had to be one of her relatives that came there in memory of her. It was Eastertime and it might have been her birthday.

When the kids were pulling on it and breaking it, I asked them to leave it alone. I told them, "That is Laura. We don't want to kill the tree. We want the tree to stay here in memory of her. That tree represents Laura Matthews. She was born in 1978 and was killed in 1980-something. The block was a part of planting that tree in her memory."

For three or four weeks, they all would come by if they saw me on the stoop and talk to me about that tree.

One Sunday afternoon my niece, Nina, my sister, Vera, and my sister's husband, Bill, had gone with Wendy and me for a walk. We came back here to the house and we were sitting on our stoop taking pictures. My daughter had just come back from Tokyo and she had one of the latest styles of cameras from Tokyo. Here came this character from toward Seventh Avenue. I was taking the pictures. I'm not good at handling cameras. So Wendy was telling me what to do. He came by and said, "Let me do it." He went to snatch it, so I snatched it back from him.

My brother-in-law was sitting across the street on the wall in front of the school, but he wasn't going to do anything anyway. Charles and three or four of the guys were sitting in front of 147 up the block.

I said, "Call the police." Charles came down with the baseball bat they had sitting there and said, "Don't come one more step closer. You better get out of here!"

He took off. You could see him flying toward Mount Morris Park. So that is how we saved that camera; the tree people didn't allow anybody to do anything in this block. They were the policemen in this block.

I worked at Olympia & York after Nabisco Brands went to New Jersey. Sometimes I worked late. I mostly came home in a taxi. Somebody would watch out for me; usually it was Charles.

"All right, Mrs. Jones, I see you," he'd say. So it has been nice.

My next project was to get the community back, because there was no sense in working on the house until you got the community stabilized. A lot of young people came through, and I was the instigator of a lot of young people getting a home. They had never seen an open brownstone until I let them into this one. That gave them the courage and incentive to buy one.

The first thing that was stolen was the stoop from 143 in '77. Scavengers stole the stoop, which was part of the six Kimball houses. I came home one evening from work and the stoop was gone. That upset me. I didn't know as much about the Kimball houses as I know now, but I didn't want to lose one of them.

One of the guys said, "Mrs. Jones, they said it was the city."

"That was not the city that took that stoop. I'm going to give you my phone number at work. Anytime you see anybody coming and looking around at these houses and taking something, you call me. I'll call the precinct. They are thieves. We have lost this stoop. Let's not lose anything else."

He said they would do that.

When houses became vacant, that is when the scavengers would come along and steal the wrought iron and the architectural ornaments off the houses. They just stole Harlem blind.

So when the tree people saw the city coming, they would go ask what they were doing. When they saw the city coming looking at one of the other houses, they told me that the city was going to demolish the house. Instead, we finally got the house fixed, because I went to Community Board 10.

The city wasn't supposed to knock down any building until they consulted Community Board 10. I went to Miss Rodman, the head of Board 10, and told her that now that the stoop had been taken down, the city was going to come back and knock the building down.

"We are saving this block because it is a great block. Don't put another hole in it. I can't stand it."

She looked at it and said, "Mrs. Jones, I'll see what we can do."

There were no faxes then, so she wrote letters and called and told them not to knock down any more buildings in this block. The city came and said they would stabilize it, since the top part was gone. I saved two houses before that.

It was in the eighties when they were going to demolish these houses. Mayor Koch was angry. As soon as one house got vacant, was not closed up, and was property that the city owned, he would just knock it down.

In the house next door to my house, the squatters had gone in and stolen everything. We had been calling the precinct about the drug people. Mayor Koch was going to knock it down, too. Ann Thomas, a community activist, told me about that. That is when I went to Miss Rodman again. She interceded in that too and stopped the city from knocking down that building. Then we had to get the drug dealers out. They were going to take over the vacant house.

This is how the city got involved with it. The homeowner had gone into a nursing home and her daughter would not see about it correctly. I had a difficult time with the daughter. She didn't want any part of the community and she wanted no part of that house.

The precinct and all the people around there were just great to work with until we got the squatters out of there. We finally got the daughter to close it up. The first time it wasn't closed up properly. The squatters went back in. Then we got her to cinder-block it. We still had to fight to keep them from going in through the roof. They still found a way in, and ended up stealing the stuff and selling it anyway.

They finally renovated that other large apartment building on Seventh Avenue and the corner of 122nd Street, which had been vacant 30 years; three developers had been in there. The people would take the construction money, do something else with it, and go away. Now that it is completed, it has stores at the bottom and residences at the top.

That building was saved because of the people in the community caring about it and letting the leaders, one of which was me, know what was going on so we could get it to the right sources. This is how we were able to bring 122nd Street back.

I had trees put in through the block association. I couldn't get more than about six trees in the block because the homeowners would not sign for me to put more trees in.

When Wendy did the research on the neighborhood, she found out that condominiums were going to be built in the vacant brownstone houses next to us. I was excited to welcome these new young people to the community.

They were all working downtown. Together we would be able to do an awful lot.

Most of them had moved in by Christmastime in '94; I had made up a package. I told them where everything was in the neighborhood, the precinct telephone number, the best places to shop, the cleaners, and the churches that were around here. I gave them all of the information that I had so they could survive in the community. I told them the parking days and what days the Department of Sanitation picked up the garbage.

When I first moved here, the garbage was picked up every day except Monday. But then they changed it to Tuesdays, Thursdays, and Saturdays. I told them to put out the garbage the night before, because they came early in the morning.

The next thing that I did was to give a tea and invite them to my house to try to get the people from the neighborhood to come meet them. I wrote them invitations and gave them two dates to choose from. Whichever got the most response was the one we would have it on. It was the first Sunday in April in 1995.

I tried to get the people on the block to come. I was disappointed that not all of them came, but I was glad that most of them came. I did invite the woman who ran the community center. This is before June of '95 when the incident happened and she put her fist in my face. She came, but I couldn't get any of the older homeowners to come. I invited tenants, too, but only two tenants came. The old preacher came. We had a good time; we bonded. Michael Henry Adams came and told them about what the houses had been through and how they had become condos.

We had a nice time, and one lady brought some food. I could see there was some tension there. The head of the community organization wanted to become the block association. The new people wanted me to give her all of my information so that she could be the block association. I told them I couldn't do that because I worked too hard and I owned my home. So I left them alone.

We had meetings once or twice. The new people would come to the meetings, and then they decided to stop coming. So I just stopped bothering. I could still get what I wanted done. This is how it ended up in conflict.

I'm not discouraged; I will keep fighting. I will get to the bottom of why they used my name in the block association after I was no longer a part of it.

A man over there was selling his drugs; I don't know what it was. I saw him taking some of the money and going. So I told him, "Don't come to this block no more."

He said, "All right, ma'am. I'm sorry."

I didn't see him out there no more. He might have come at night, but not when I could see him. What they do is when they can't go in one neighborhood, they go into another.

I don't know of any other block that has made such a comeback. Because of my house, a great number of people from Europe and all different parts of the country have been here. I have letters from them. I have given them information about Harlem that they had never heard of. This is how this block really got on the map. The houses have been publicized in magazines, on radio, and television.

Preservation means that you don't destroy; you preserve. They are into painting the buildings red and knocking down the stoops. If we don't preserve history for our children, then we won't have it; it won't be there.

When the tour driver and the tour buses pass through here, they know me; they look for me. I wave at the tourists. People stop and talk to me. It is a warm feeling. We do have something that people want to see. It is the façade that they come by to see, and the atmosphere of the block is livable. The tourists don't understand why nobody is hanging on the stoop in this block, but it wasn't always like this.

People were hanging in the street. They were dealing drugs. They were doing everything that they wanted to do in this block because nobody in the block cared. Somebody has to care. You have to keep fighting. It didn't happen overnight.

Yes, I had help with my men; those men are gone now. Some have died and some have moved away. We got more people in here than the block ever had because of the new houses. Hopefully, we can bond with them. A lot of it has to do with the homeowners who themselves don't do anything. The homeowners have to set the example for the tenants, and hopefully they will get it done. We are not discouraged.

The school custodians are putting the garbage out in front of the school. We have to work on that. It needs to be in the back. I hope by next spring, I'll have it done.

CHAPTER 13

WORKING AT OLYMPIA & YORK

The Reichmann family, born in Vienna, fled the Nazis during WWII and finally made it to Tangier, Morocco, where the successful merchant father, Samuel, groomed three of his six sons for business careers. Eventually, they settled in Canada, where one brother's tile business morphed into a construction company that became known for innovative and economical building techniques. With the addition of another brother's real estate company, the three brothers, Paul, Albert, and Ralph, formed the company that became known as Olympia & York in 1969.

By the time they opened their 237 Park Avenue office in New York in 1982, the Reichmanns were famous for building a 72-story office building, the tallest building *in Canada at that time, First Canadian Place, which resulted in a profit of US $1 billion.*

They also bought a block of eight office buildings in Manhattan, known as the Uris project, later valued at $3 billion, and won the right to construct the World Financial Center. The center was a deal worth over $300 million. Both in Canada and in the United States the brothers bought at basement prices during a time of economic hardship, then property values skyrocketed during the prosperous times.

Following Orthodox Jewish practice, all work on their construction sites stopped at sundown on Fridays in observance of the Sabbath and on all Jewish holy days. The Reichmanns sealed their deals with handshakes rather than contracts and were known to be ethical in all their business dealings. In 1986 my mother went to work for them.

A friend had given my name to Olympia & York because the company had a kosher kitchen. They wanted to hire a consultant so they could get some real food to eat. I went down there for two weeks and did a survey to see what we needed to bring it up to standard.

Olympia & York was the biggest commercial real estate company in New York. They came into New York

City in 1976. The newspapers said, "The quiet man buys up half of the real estate of Battery Park." They called Mr. Paul Reichmann the quiet man because he used few words, but he got what he wanted, which was money from all these banks and all the real estate property that he wanted. He had everything under his control here in New York as far as real estate was concerned.

All they had was a cleaning woman. She came from National Cleaning. She didn't have any expertise in doing anything with food, even ordering. I asked her would she be willing to be trained, but she would have to come over on O&Y's payroll. She said no, she wasn't interested in it. There has never been a cleaning person who had the skills to become a food handler.

Then we started looking for somebody. We hired somebody to come for three days; she only lasted three days. She was looking for a job where she didn't have to do any work. This wasn't a job that had four or five people on staff; you were it.

They agreed to keep me on part-time after they had such a hard time finding anyone to do the job. I worked there for about a month by myself, getting help from the temporary agencies. It was actually too much for one person.

They had meetings around the clock. There was always some food to be served. Olympia & York had fifteen different executives. Anytime they rang the bell, you gave them coffee from the kitchen. Then you had to serve it, which made it almost impossible to get the lunch ready, because somebody always wanted something. But we did get it under control, because I hired a permanent person from eight to four.

It was a great company to work for. They paid good money. They gave me car service to and from the office for a month after I went back to work when I had surgery. And they gave good bonuses at Christmastime.

But I could see they were headed for destruction, because nobody was in control. I've never seen money spent like that money was spent. I asked the executives did they have a budget. They didn't even know what a budget was.

One of the secretaries, René, worked for Mr. Paul Reichmann.

I said to her, "René, you better save some of your money." She was a person who wore a new outfit every day. She could go for a month and not have on the same outfit.

"You're making good money now. But this isn't going to last."

"Oh yes, Mrs. Jones. They're millionaires. They'll always be rich. I don't save money, Mrs. Jones. I don't have a bank account."

"How can you survive?" I think she was just turning 50 that year.

"What do you think is going to happen to you? When this runs out, where are you going? You'll never find another job like this, because they're not out there now. And you won't have anything but your unemployment. Don't you know you have to save?"

"Mama keeps telling me that, too, but I don't bother about saving. I just spend it all."

"What about your daughter, Maureen?"

"She spends it all, too. We have two or three closets already, but we just had another closet built so we could put in more clothes."

"René, do me a favor. Next week when you get paid, open up a savings account. Put so much money in every payday. You get paid every week. Put at least 25 or 30 dollars in it. I don't know what your salary is. Maybe you could save a hundred dollars a week. Put it in there. And you had better get you some CDs and some kind of annuities or something. If you don't, you won't have anything when you get old."

"I'm paying into the pension plan."

"A pension plan has never been a salary."

So she went and started saving herself some money.

After I retired, I ran into Fred, who had been working for Office Canteen. He was working for another company. I met him when I was working at O&Y. He was coming into that building because he was the manager of one of the cafeterias there.

"Oh, Mrs. Jones."

"Yes."

"What are you doing here? I thought you—"

"I did retire, but I'm working as a consultant for O&Y; they own this building."

His company had a cafeteria on the 14th floor. "Now, I understand what you meant when we came into your place."

"Uh-huh, the shoe is on the other foot."

"I can appreciate how you felt now. I feel just like you felt and I do the same things that you talked about."

Their company was bought out by Office Service from Europe. They did him like they tried to do me. So he had to leave. Those employees that didn't get fired, left.

"You should have seen them, Mrs. Jones."

"I told you. It doesn't last."

I think Office Service is out of business now, too.

Sometimes we might feed a hundred or two hundred people a day, because everybody knew O&Y had a great lunch. It was out in the industry: make your meetings for lunchtime and you would get a good lunch. Sometimes we had lunch for 10, 15, 20 or 25 people. And this was every day!

Sometimes they'd come in at ten o'clock and say they wanted lunch for 12 people because they were going to stay through lunch. Then you would have to order more food. The kitchen wasn't large enough for a kosher kitchen. If it had been large enough, it would have been fine. Then you would have had space on each side to keep food separately.

But there wasn't enough working space to keep the meat and dairy separate. You didn't have anywhere to put anything. You are not supposed to sit the meat dishes on the dairy side of the refrigerator, and the dairy dishes are not supposed to sit on the meat side. You have to have one shelf for the meat and one shelf for the dairy. You needed a big kitchen where you could have a refrigerator for the dairy and a refrigerator for the meat. You also needed one side of the room for the dairy dishes and one side for the meat dishes. Two kitchens would have been even better.

Although I had worked for Jewish people, I had never worked for a kosher Jewish person. But I'd always read a lot about what they did and how they did it. The company also sent me to kosher food preparation training classes. I knew how to handle the food, and there was a rabbi for the kitchen. The things I was in doubt about, I would call and ask him. We had a dairy place and a meat place to order the food from. You always ordered dairy items for breakfast. There was never meat when there was dairy. For lunch, you just didn't bother with the dairy folks. If you were having meat, you got it from Siegel's. And that was it.

They took a lot out of you. I worked there sometimes 14 or 15 hours. Mr. Paul Reichmann knew no limits. He was like a clock; he just kept ticking and going around.

The secretary had to stay with him, and she wanted me to stay with her. He would have to have tea or something every half hour or every five minutes sometimes. I always stayed with her, but I was always sent home by car when I stayed late.

On this particular project, they went over to London to Canary Wharf. Even my church was involved with Canary Wharf. Second Presbyterian, and the Presbytery itself, had lost a whole lot of money investing in the project. One of our church members, who was an employee at First Boston, was working on it.

At first, Olympia & York couldn't get enough backers to develop Canary Wharf. It was like a little island. They had to build a subway and a railroad and a trestle for the place so people could get from there back to London. They were going to make Canary Wharf the most exquisite thing in London.

Olympia & York were going over there to get all the backers. They were going to leave at five o'clock Sunday morning. Since they were Orthodox, they couldn't do anything on a Saturday. They had their private plane. They had to have lunch and it had to be fixed in a kosher place. So they came to me and asked what are we going to do and how are we going to do it.

I said, "Well, just like we can build Canary Wharf, I can get food on the plane. I'll get the food in, come down here one o'clock Sunday morning, make the lunch, and have the chauffeur pick it up. Simple as that."

Mr. Paul was amazed. He came out and said, "Jo, you—"

"Sure. It's your responsibility to build the buildings for Canary Wharf, and you'll find a way to do it. And I'll find a way to get food where it's supposed to go."

I told my sister Vera to come spend the night with me, because I didn't want to be in that building by myself. We went down there and fixed the lunch; the chauffeur came, got it, and put it on the plane.

But I said that this would be Mr. Paul's last project, and it was. He went over there and was going to build, but could not get the backers to invest in it.

Citibank and the others had lent him so much money. They said he didn't have a thing to do but walk into any bank, talk to their investment people, cross his legs, and he had a million dollars.

Olympia & York went bankrupt completely in the United States and in Canada, so now he's completely out of the United States. I think they still have one building in Canada. Canary Wharf is under whole new management. Citibank was trying to fix it—I don't know how many millions of dollars they had lent him—so they could get their money out of it.

I heard that he went down to Mexico to build some buildings. I guess he'll find the backers down there. Of course, he has plenty of money. Olympia & York's money was never invested in the buildings; it was the banks that were losing. So they're still millionaires.

But there again, people don't look and see what's going on. You could see there was no way in the world it could last. You had a whole lot of people that worked there who went out and started their own real estate firms.

It was a good job. I did very well there and was very well liked. But I expected it to end.

I left O&Y in April of '89. That was when I really got involved in restoring the house. I had put everything on hold when I went to work for O&Y.

CHAPTER 14

RESTORING THE BROWNSTONE

As soon as she moved in, March 1976, my mother began working on the house. With the help of friends, she removed the sheetrock partition and moved into the master bedroom on the second floor. Mama also removed a partition and a sink from the back parlor on the first above-ground floor, The house was livable, although not yet restored. When my mother returned to Citibank to borrow money to restore the house, the bank still refused to lend her any money.

When I left Olympia & York, I decided I would get involved with the restoration. When Big Ma was alive, I always went home during my vacation time to see her. But after she passed, I started using my resources for restoration projects on the house. I thought that I could find the craftsmen who were interested in the house, wanted to do the work, and *could* do the work.

I started calling numbers from different ads. That is the worst way to get craftsmen. The best way is to get craftsmen recommended by someone or you see their work.

For example, the local plumber, Mr. Anderson, had been working with me a long time. But I found out that he and his crew weren't doing anything; nothing ever got finished.

That's what happened to the entranceway, which was supposed to have been restored. Thousands of dollars went into it, and it's not been finished properly. That was because I didn't have the expertise. I didn't know what to demand. You pay for your mistakes.

Then I got involved with the carpenter with the kitchen. I knew some things that needed to be done, but I was told that it couldn't be done. For instance, the flooring, which is tongue and groove, I knew that a machine should be able to cut it. However, the carpenter kept insisting that there were no machines that cut lumber to order, no plants around to do it. I read an awful lot in the different magazines that said it could be done.

He had a little electrical handsaw. He bought the lumber in bulk and was going to cut it to size. He spent four or five hours cutting enough to do maybe two feet or three feet. Anyway, I was getting annoyed with him because he was using up more of my money for labor than anything getting done. Then his father died and he had to go away for a while.

I took a piece of the flooring and the lumber and went down to a place at 33rd Street on 11th Avenue. I asked them if lumber could be cut to size. I told them what the carpenter had said.

The man walked me through his factory. He built the most beautiful cabinets you ever wanted to see, all kinds of designs. He also showed me the spray place where they sprayed the cabinets after they had been made and the computer room where any wood could be cut to size.

When the carpenter came back, I just told him to leave.

These are the things that you get involved in because you don't understand and you don't know. You meet people who take advantage of you. I lost a lot, but I'll recoup from that and move on.

In the meantime, we had the problem with the ailanthus trees growing out of the brownstone. Seeds had been blown there by the wind, and they pushed some of the bricks out. The trees were really growing out of the house next door, but it's hard to see where one of these houses begins and the other ends So here came the Environmental Protection Agency, who started giving me violations.

I had to leave the work I was having done on the inside of the house and go to the outside of the house. I also had a leak; I was getting wet every time it rained, so I knew I needed roof work. There was no sense in fixing the inside until I got a better roof on it.

I could have had the house fixed I don't know how many times—and it wouldn't have been that expensive. But we didn't have the craftspeople to do the job correctly. Wendy and I had driven around and looked at some of the work. We checked the different companies that sent out brochures. We even checked one in New Jersey. I'd gone to enough seminars to know that it wasn't quality restoration.

Seminars were given by the Brownstone Revival Committee and Landmarks Conservancy. Every year they gave a seminar on the interior or the exterior or the plumbing or the windows. I'd been attending those since 1976 when I bought the house. I did meet a lot of craftsmen there.

But then what happened? When they found out that I lived in Harlem, they just wouldn't come. They'd make an appointment and they didn't even call to cancel. And these are the craftsmen from the restoration people. So this is one of the reasons why a lot of the work is still hanging and was never done.

I would always save articles pertaining to restoration. An article in '81 came out in the *New York Times*. It was entitled "Help for Old Buildings." It talked about getting help for any building built before 1930, for the exterior. By the time I called, it was 1990. I called and asked was this offer still standing.

The first guy that got ahold of me said that there wasn't any help because I was not in a Landmark district. "Well, I'm not in the district; I'm over from it. But I'm not asking for grants. I'm asking for someone to help me get the craftsmen to come to Harlem, because for me alone, they won't come."

"Let me give you to Mr. Ed Rand and see what he can do."

Mr. Rand said to me, "I don't know, but from the way you describe that building, it's a building that the National Trust for Historic Preservation would put on the list. If they do that, then we can give you the loan. But you have to have research work done on it. I'll come through and look at it."

He came out and looked at the building. Then he told me to call Ms. Hess, who worked at the Parks Department, and ask for an application to get the house listed on the National Register of Historic Places, so that I would be able to get a loan.

She sent me out this huge application that looked like you needed a PhD in architecture to fill it out. I was kind of baffled about it. Wendy and I didn't really know what to do with it. Then I went to a seminar at the Polk Building. I think it was on the interior of brownstones. But anyway, I saw Margaret Gayle; she was the one who started the city saving the cast-iron buildings and the cast-iron railings. I asked her if she knew where I could get any help.

"There goes Marjorie Pearson; she's the research director for the Landmark Commission of Harlem." Marjorie gave me her card and told me to call her.

When I called her she told me, "Yes, we looked at those buildings when we landmarked Mount Morris. I have the history of your building. I will send it to you."

For some unknown reason they did not landmark the area over to Seventh Avenue. They discontinued it at Lenox Avenue and Mount Morris Park from 119th Street to 124th Street, and from Mount Morris Park to Lenox

Avenue on the west side. So our group of houses was not included in it.

Fred Williams had introduced himself to me and given me his card. He said I might need his help. This was approximately 1991. I called Mr. Williams and asked him if he could come help me fill out this application.

We didn't need all the information that they said we needed. It just went one, two, three. We sent the information and the pictures of the neighborhood and the building to the National Historic Registry up there in Albany. It was around Christmastime when we got the notice back that it had been put on the National Historic Registry, so the house was eligible for the loan. Then going through the process of applying took another year.

Some of the delay was due to death in the family. I lost my oldest brother. We were due to close on the loan on April 15, 1992. My brother died on the 11th of April, so we had to put that back so I could go to the funeral.

January 15, 1993, we finally got it. When I talked to Cahill, the person at the agency in charge of processing the loan, a couple of days ago about the second loan, I asked him, "Why do I have to wait another year to process the loan to restore the windows?" He said, "You know how long it takes the loan to go through the application process." I can't understand why it takes all this time now.

It looks like it would just be an add-on. The information is already there.

The first loan was just enough to do the façade and the roof. That's what's so expensive about this building. There are so many different categories of architectural work. When I finish the windows, I still have the stained glass, which is another expense.

Cahill says it's going to take about nine hundred dollars a window. But I'm still arguing, because some of the windows here are smaller than the others. It looks like the large windows would be nine hundred and the small windows would be five hundred. These are the things we're going to have to try to work out.

But it's frustrating because we don't seem to be able to get the resources and the craftsmen together on our own, which means we have to be involved with so many different people. You never know whether you're getting the right people or not. I didn't realize it would be this detailed, as involved as it is. But I'm not giving up.

The dream for the house is for it to be an incentive for the children of our culture, something they can feel, touch, and see. I want the house to be an educational tool for them while I am living, and then I can pass it on to Wendy.

When you look at this building, you see all the crafts from the different craftsmen. Our children are not exposed to that. I don't know if they think a building just gets there by itself, but all this is the work of man. The designing of it, the plastering of it, the tiles and fireplace, all this came from men—and from women too, now.

By the time they are 18, 19, or 20 years old, and they say they're going to become an architect, they don't know the foundation of it. I wanted to be able to let them come in and have craftsmen to explain to them that they too can build and design their own homes. And design for other people, too.

I think if our children knew what these buildings consisted of, they wouldn't destroy our things. If they knew the beauty of it, and the history of it, and the art part of it, they wouldn't destroy our community. They would want to save it and preserve it.

What the children don't realize is that in our culture we were builders. But if you don't have anybody to tell you what black people did, you won't know about it. These are the things we want to involve our children in. I also want to stress the importance of preserving your health.

I have a profession of my own I would like to teach the children, the young women and the young men, about how we can take care of our bodies. I have found that prevention is the best way to stay healthy.

I think about myself; I'm one of the few people my age, 74, who is not on some form of medication. That came from eating right from the beginning. I don't know what my mother fed us.

The people in the South had good food. But it was something we didn't want, because we had plenty of it. We thought if we went to the store, it would be better. We grew our own vegetables and we had our own chickens, pigs, and cows.

We went to the store and bought our bread, and we thought that bread was the best bread we ever had in our lives, but it wasn't. We were already eating the best bread; our mothers cooked it. But we thought if we went to the store, oh, we had something new. We got a loaf of what we called light bread. It wasn't even sliced; you pulled it off.

I want to teach the children to take care of themselves, their health, in the beginning of life. We don't have to have chemicals to keep our body together. It's the food that we need.

Let's go back to our roots, our architecture, and our crafts: our needlework and embroidery. We are the ones who created the setting of tables, which has become a lost art to us. We don't know what fork to use.

I want to leave that legacy here. I want them to know that things can be done. You have to work a little harder or go to another resource to get things done. There's been a lot of money made out of quilting, but we're not making it. Who's out there quilting quilts? The slaves were the ones that made all the quilts. It's not well known among the general public. People think we didn't do it, because we're not out there doing it now. But I still have the knowledge of what my mother taught us to do, and it can be taught. I want to leave it here for future generations.

I was able to walk into the unknown through Wendy's work. I think she is the backbone of all of this. Because if it had not been for her, I don't think I ever would have wanted a house. Or maybe I never would've had to have one. I think I would've been a great traveler. But after becoming a mother, I knew there was something I had to establish, something for my daughter.

I set about to develop myself and get her to develop the things that she could do, so she could be a person. I'm blessed and I'm happy. There is nothing in the world that I would give for her not being part of me. Out of the marriage and out of the headaches and the joy and the pain—the joy was Wendy. The pain doesn't matter anymore. It was my daughter that came out of this—partnership, as she calls it. I called it marriage then, but now I call it partnership.

I look at her as just the other half of me. I know we are two people, but when you see something grow and develop and you know that you developed this, it's a great feeling. Nothing takes the place of it. I see people looking for glory out here. I have mine.

I have no regrets. I don't want Wendy to ever feel that I have regrets for working three jobs for her; it was what I wanted to do, so she could be a person. I would never have had to work three jobs if the system had been set up so that we would have been able to survive.

It didn't bother me, because I could do it. The point is that I got results from it. I don't know how I would've felt if I hadn't got results from it. But I knew all along that I had a tree that would grow if I gave it the right fertilizer. So that was what I was going to do. If it took three jobs or four jobs to do it, I was going to let this tree have the right fertilizer. We can't say we can't do anything, because I know that all things can be done if we get good opportunities and we're at the right place at the right time.

I just saw in the papers—I'm going to speak to Cahill about it when I see him Thursday—where they gave a ten thousand dollar grant to some woman in Brooklyn, and I want to know why they can't give me a grant. What is wrong? It didn't seem that her house was in the Landmark area. And the grant came from the Landmark Conservancy.

I have been in the newsletter. If I don't restore one of Kimball's houses in this area, it will never be restored.

I do believe that I'm the only black or white woman here in Harlem who has a house and is restoring it. Everybody else who has a brownstone has made apartments out of it. They have the living room and the kitchen for themselves, on this floor, the parlor floor. And the other two floors are made into apartments. They got these houses for a business.

Nothing good ever comes to you overnight. I should know that. But I do think there should be some grants around that I could tap into. It looks like someone would want to see the wrought iron put back. But I guess I don't know the right folks. People seem to help people who got. But you should help the person who's struggling. I think that's why I don't get any recognition in the organizations I belong to, because they don't know me. If you can say you have a PhD and you're a teacher and all of this—then you become somebody. I shouldn't be discouraged. It's just sometimes it gets so overwhelming.

The reason I'm so involved with children is that when children come in here—they don't understand this is a house. They're looking to see who lives upstairs. To them, it must be an apartment building. Where's my kitchen? To them this is the apartment. I have to keep telling them it's a house.

One morning—this is when I was still working—a child and his mother were passing while I was waiting for the bus. He must have been about four or five years old. He stopped and looked at Mickey's Funeral Home, which is in a brownstone over there; he was just admiring that building. He wanted a house like that. Instead of her telling him that someday, if you go to school and get your education, you can have a building like that, she said, "Where you think you going to get that building from? You ain't going to never get anything like that. Come on here."

I wanted to talk to the child, but I couldn't. I wanted to tell him, "You're on the road now. You go to school. You learn, you get yourself an education, and you can own that building or one like that building. Maybe you wouldn't want one like that. You could design and build your own building."

There right in the beginning of his little life, he's told he can't do it. These are the things that we need to say to a young child who asks questions like that. Tell them

293

what they can do to become that person that they want to be, own what they see out there and be a part of it. But when you don't have any hope yourself, you certainly aren't going to give your children any.

Out of all the courses I have taken, and all the seminars I've been to in food, I have yet to have a black instructor, which means we've been left out of it. I want to bring us back into it.

Everywhere you go, people are complaining. "This is hurting," and "My blood pressure is up." And you look at them and you can tell why, because they have eaten themselves to death. I don't think they know what to eat. If it tastes good, they just eat it and eat it all. We have to know there's another way to do things.

There's a lot to be learned from me as a black woman. Once people know my life story, they'll know that I did accomplish an awful lot.

EPILOGUE

SINGING HARLEM'S SONG

Mama had appeared in a New Yorker *article with the architectural historian, Michael Henry Adams, discussing Small's Paradise. The writer of the article recommended her to George C. Wolfe, who was looking for community residents to interview.*

On August 4, 2002, Harlem Song, *written and directed by George C. Wolfe, opened at the Apollo in Harlem. This musical showcased Harlem's history from the black migration to the present through song, dance, and interviews with neighborhood people. My mother was one of the interviewees.*

Frenetic and MTV-like in its pace, dancing and singing intertwined while interviews flashed by. I glimpsed Mama's white, wide-brimmed Easter parade hat. Then she talked about Harlem when she first came to New York: "The men wore three-piece suits and there was music everywhere. On June 14, 1952, I met Wendy's father at the Savoy. The marriage didn't last, but the music did."

Although it was my first time seeing the show, my mother had seen it several times. The night of her birthday, Mama went with Michael Adams and an East Indian tourist from Canada. The Canadian tourist had a fine time with my mother. He said he enjoyed her authenticity. After the show was over, Michael introduced her to the audience. "Here is the woman who was in the show. This is Mrs. Jones, and today is her birthday. I think it would be very nice if we all sang 'Happy Birthday' to her." *The entire audience sang to Mama that night.*

The summer night I saw Harlem Song *I could feel the electricity crackling between the audience and the cast. My mother sat next to me in her black chiffon dress and her black picture hat, proud and happy.*

After it was over, a woman in the theater lobby recognized Mama and took a picture with her. Rushing to catch the subway, I looked back and saw my mother on the sidewalk outside of the Apollo. A small circle of people had gathered around her, long fingers gesturing in the spill of the marquee light as the black hat framed her face, Mama was holding court, her rolling voice saying: "I came to New York in 1946 . . ."

APPENDIX

HOW MAMA NURTURED MY EDUCATION

When Mama finished her life story, I realized something was missing. She had said nothing about all she had done to nurture my education. It was not like my mother to talk about how much she had done for me. However, Mama's focus on my education was an important part of her story.

ALEXANDER ROBERTSON SCHOOL

I had a rich and vibrant education both in and out of schools, but before my trip around the world, before Japan, before Columbia, Yale, Dalton, and Alexander Robertson, there was Mama.

For as far back as I can remember, I had seen my mother reading. Most often it was the *Daily News* during the week and the *Daily News* and the *New York Times* on Sunday. Mama subscribed to *Reader's Digest* and

McCall's magazine. After I went off to college, she enrolled in evening courses at Pace College and Baruch College. My mother wrote a paper on the Federalist Papers and enjoyed discussing Faulkner's *Light in August*.

One summer I took books out of the library for the two of us. That's how we discovered the short stories of Somerset Maugham. Soon after reading one of Maugham's short story collections, we saw the movie adaptation of *The Letter*, starring Bette Davis. I sat on the light green-carpeted floor in front of the bed while Mama sat in bed dressed in a white lace slip with her back up against the headboard. For once, we both agreed, the movie was almost as good as the story.

When I was in second grade, school testing revealed that I was reading on an eighth-grade level. Shortly after that, I wanted to take a book out of the public library that was considered an adult book. I don't remember which book it was.

When the librarian told me I couldn't take the book out, my mother told the librarian that I had her permission. However, the librarian insisted it was against the rules. Mama said she felt that I should be allowed to read any book I was capable of reading. Finally, my mother took the book out on her card and gave it to me.

The summer I turned 12, I went on vacation to my adult cousin's house in Greenville, South Carolina. My cousin told me that her pornographic books were off-limits. So of course, I read them.

My mother had tearfully called my Aunt Sally, who was a nurse's aide, when my first period arrived a month after my 12th birthday. My aunt told me not to "experiment." I had no idea what she meant, but dutifully promised I wouldn't. The medical dictionary ("a young girl's first menstrual period indicates that she is now physically capable of becoming a mother") did not tell me what I wanted to know: exactly what went on during sexual intercourse. Fortunately for me, my cousin's paperbacks did.

From my mother I learned to see reading as fun, as much fun as dancing, singing, or watching television. Although Mama tells me she read to me, I don't remember that. When I was in first grade, I showed my mother I could read by reading the Macy's sales advertisement in the *Daily News*, as mentioned earlier. I read constantly after that. In fact, for a while I thought that books were born, not written.

Mama not only set the example of the importance of reading, but she also kept a sharp eye on my formal education from the very beginning.

Learning to read in first grade had been exciting, ("Read with expression," Mrs. Fanning had said), but because Mrs. Deeds (my teacher) and I shared a birthday, second grade was even better. My mother brought the same yellow cake with chocolate frosting and pink lettering that she made for my birthdays at home to our joint celebration at school. During second grade reading time I assisted the kindergarten teacher because I had finished the textbook on my own.

Mrs. Greenlee's third-grade class was pure hell. It was a year of firsts. For the first time, I had a teacher who didn't like me, and I felt the same way about her. When I told the girl behind me to stop kicking the back of my chair, I was the one who was scolded for talking.

In church, my mother discovered I couldn't see the large numbers on the sign that listed the hymnal pages, so she took me to the eye doctor.

"Has this child been walking across the street by herself?" asked the eye doctor.

"No, I guess she's been overprotected," replied Mama apologetically.

"It's a good thing. She couldn't see the cars."

My third-grade teacher never noticed that I read fluently when reading aloud from a book on my desk, but stumbled through the filmstrip captions when asked to read them, even though I was sitting in the front row. Because I could not see the blackboard until late in third grade when I started wearing glasses, I never learned the fundamentals of arithmetic.

Years later it dawned on me that my second-grade teacher had been showing our class the ones, tens, and hundreds places by putting sticks in each of three pockets she had hung on the blackboard. Unable to see what she was doing, I had drifted off into a daydream.

Third grade provided another first for me. I was with two boys in the school lobby when one of them called me a nigger. I did not know what the word meant because I had never heard it before. But I knew it was something bad from the tone of the boy's voice. I was hurt, angry, and sad. Of course, I didn't tell the teacher.

The after-school program that I attended called my mother. A staff member told her that I seemed very sad about something, that I wasn't myself.

That evening Mama asked me, "Baby, are you sick? Where does it hurt?"

"No, Mama, I'm not sick."

"What's wrong?"

Mama and I were sitting next to each other on the couch in the living room. It must have been fall, because the dark green couch with gold sparkly curlicues was covered with the gray cotton couch cover that signaled the beginning of cold weather in our home. The lamp on the end table enclosed us in a cone of light.

"Am I a nigger?"

"No, you're not. Let's get the dictionary."

The dictionary defined the word as any dirty, low, or disreputable person.

My mother explained that some people did use it to refer to us, but they were wrong. People were different colors, just like flowers. A yellow rose was no better or worse than a red rose, just different. She said that people who used the word didn't know who they were. They were the ones who had a problem. Then Mama hugged me.

When my mother discussed the incident with Mrs. Greenlee, she felt only coldness from the teacher. Mrs. Greenlee did not feel that she had anything to do with what had happened and did not express any sympathy for my feelings.

The story now takes an odd turn. Playing the scene back in my mind, I now realize that the boy who called me that name was probably also black. He had freckles, oatmeal-colored skin, gray-green eyes, and wiry reddish-brown hair. The student may have been older than I was, because his gravelly low voice was too deep for a boy in the third grade. The school went up to the sixth grade. At any rate, at that time the incident was treated as if he were white or identified as white in the school.

Much later Mama told me that it was then she knew she had to get me away from that teacher and out of the school. The way my mother saw it, these were mostly the same children I had been going to school with since kindergarten, and I had never had any problems before; the only difference was the teacher.

If Mrs. Greenlee had not created the kind of environment that made it possible for the boy to use that word, he would never have used it. Mama felt the teacher should've made a special effort to make me feel welcome, because I was the only black student in the third and fourth grades. Since both grades were taught in the same room by the same teacher, I would have had Mrs. Greenlee the next year, too.

Public school had never been an option for me. When my mother came to New York in 1946, she went to the neighborhood public school to vote. The reek of urine and the sight of graffiti-covered walls convinced Mama that no future child of hers was going to a public school in New York City. She didn't see how a child could learn anything in such filth and disorder.

During this time period I overheard my mother say that she didn't want her daughter sitting at a desk next to a white child just for the sake of sitting there. Mama wanted me at that desk so I could get the same education that white child was getting. It was then up to me to do something with that education.

My mother told me that the reason wealthy white people in America had money, power, and position was that they had stolen them. First, they had stolen the land from the Indians. Then they had stolen black people from Africa. And finally, they had stolen our labor during slavery and continued to pay us poorly as salaried workers. That was the system.

Riding the bus to work, Mama would ask public school kids and private school kids (some wore uniforms or, as in the case of Dalton, had distinctive book bags) what grade they were in. My mother saw that children in the same grade had different textbooks for the same subjects. How could they be getting the same education if they had different books? The public school books, just as hers had been, were handed down from year to year and turned back in for the next year's incoming students. The public school textbooks were also older than the books the private school children had.

Mrs. Cahan suggested Mama try to get me into Dalton. Mrs. Cahan's niece had gone there, so she knew it was a good school. Although the administrator did not remember Mrs. Cahan's sister when Mrs. Cahan mentioned the name during an exploratory phone call, there was no problem getting an interview scheduled for me.

Dalton agreed to interview me even though it was January and most of the spaces had already been filled for September. I went up to the second floor in an Otis elevator that was made of reddish-colored wood with brass trim. The elevator operator was a slim, cocoa-brown young woman wearing a black skirt, white blouse, black sweater, and white gloves. She was introduced as Miss Emily. The doors opened onto the blue-carpeted second floor where the administrative offices were located. Mama and I walked into an office where a white woman sat behind a large wooden desk lit by a banker's green-shaded desk lamp.

The administrator asked what kind of work my mother did and what I did after school. I answered the first question but not the second. All I could think of to say was that I played on the stoop near the school, but I knew she probably didn't mean that.

After that I followed another staff person, probably a psychologist, into another room where I drew a picture of a girl hanging out the window of an attic. She was looking at some boys who were going to play baseball. When asked to talk about the picture, I explained that the boys wouldn't let her play because she was a girl. I didn't tell the woman that the boys were my cousins.

When the interviewer asked me what was in the attic, I told her that there were lots of chairs: little ones, big ones, soft ones, and hard ones. My mother and I had gone to visit Mama's supervisor, Mrs. Dunfield. This is the apartment that my mother would later clean out. At that time, a person could still walk around in it. Mrs. Dunfield and her sister collected all kinds of chairs. They kept them in the living room, which made the room look like a small theater. Looking back, I wonder what deep psychological interpretation my drawing was given.

In a few weeks, the person in Dalton's admissions office called to say that although I was a very good possibility for the school, there was no space available this year; I was invited to reapply the next year. Mama told me not to feel bad about not being accepted. She thought maybe the people were too wealthy and I would not have been comfortable there.

Maybe a week later, there was another call from Dalton asking me to come for another interview, because someone had dropped off the waiting list. I don't remember the second interview, but that fall I started fourth grade at Dalton.

The principal, Dr.Kittell, offered me a full scholarship. However, my mother responded that she would pay half of my tuition so that she could have a say in my education. Mama told the principal that it was the system that made it impossible for her to make enough money to pay full tuition. My mother paid her half of my tuition with income from her three jobs.

The principal told her that, as wealthy as they were, none of the other parents would have turned down a full scholarship. He also let my mother know that if there was ever a trip or event that the class was attending and she couldn't afford it, the school would pay for it.

DALTON

Transferring to Dalton from Alexander Robertson was, in some ways, the equivalent of the country mouse going to visit her city cousin, and in others, it was a perfect fit. Mama had laid the groundwork for my love of learning. My mother had also given me practice in how to organize my time. From the time I was about seven years old, Mama had given me responsibilities in the house. My weekly routine included cleaning the bathroom and dusting the living room. These tasks echoed the pattern of responsibilities I would be asked to undertake at Dalton. I thrived in the yeasty environment of good teaching, flexibility, and structure that was Dalton.

A lot of subjects were taught differently at Dalton. For instance, the year before in my third-grade class at Alexander Robertson, the class was drilled in addition and subtraction through the use of timed worksheets on paper so old it was brown around the edges and cotton fibers appeared when students erased mistakes.

Meanwhile, Dalton's third-grade class had set up a classroom store. In the store they priced items, bought and sold them to each other, and made change. Dalton's students were learning basic arithmetic using a hands-on creative method while Alexander Robertson's students were learning the same subject using nineteenth-century rote methods.

An even greater difference in teaching methods between the two schools was the Dalton Plan, a modified Montessori method, in which students were given monthly assignments broken into four weeks. Students could choose their own projects or papers from a list of suggestions, but agreed to follow the "contract" and complete their work on time.

At the end of the month, teachers signed students' unit cards to show that they had completed all the work.

This was called being "off" your assignment. The question we would ask each other on the last Friday of the fourth week of the month was, "Are you off?" We could get extensions on our assignments, but then we would have to do the old work as well as the new.

My fourth-grade teacher was a kindhearted, white-haired woman named Linda, but I refused to call Mrs. Schiller by her first name. My teacher was old enough to be my grandmother.

A Dalton education started, in those days, at two years old. Many of the children in my class had been together since they were two, and socialized outside of school. There were many cliques. The most powerful one was run by Rachel and Susan. They had a group of so-called friends who did what they were told.

"How many years have you been trying to get into Dalton?" Susan asked.

"Just one," I answered in surprise.

Another day Susan wanted to know, "Why don't you call Linda by her name like everybody else does?"

"Her name is Mrs. Schiller. It's not polite to call your teacher by her first name."

"But everybody else does," Susan persisted.

"I don't."

One morning while walking to the bus stop for school with my Uncle Calvin, I asked him about it. He agreed with me.

Despite the fact that Mama worked outside of the home and most of the other mothers did not, she joined the costume committee as her contribution to the school community. She made the olive-green brocade dress for the lead actress in the high school's production of "The Madwoman of Chaillot."

After-school activities kept me busy. Dalton offered ice-skating at Wollman's rink in Central Park and bowling at an alley near the school in the winter. In the spring, there was baseball at Randall's Island.

I had a set schedule. After arriving at home around six, I took a nap. I had dinner at seven, then did homework on the dining room table from eight until midnight. Often, my mother would call out from her bedroom next to the dining room at 11 p.m., "Wendy, it's late. Go to bed!"

I always answered, "I can sleep in the summer!"

Once Mama's entanglement with a sister's problems affected me at school. In fifth grade I ran, with a group of other students, giggling out of my homeroom, which was called my "house" in the language of Dalton, calling my teacher by the dreaded nickname of "Pottyman." Mr. Portmann, a young teacher, probably in his mid-twenties, needed to establish his authority with us. He had told us not to call him that. He followed me to the staircase.

"Wendy, I'm surprised. You usually don't do things like this. Now, what's the matter?" he asked, sitting down on the stair step beside me.

"The others did it, too. You didn't run after them."

"I'm not concerned about the others. I'm talking about you. We're going to sit here until you tell me why you did this. There must be something wrong."

I stalled as long as I could, but the second bell had rung and I was going to be late for math. I hadn't been thinking about it, but I had to tell him something. It burst out of me like a firecracker exploding.

"My mother's giving money to my aunt, and I'm afraid we'll run out of money." Then I started crying.

I didn't know all the details then, but I had overheard another phone call about another aunt in need of a loan. Later I found out that when my Aunt Maude separated from her spouse, she and her children were in danger of losing their house. My mother and Aunt Vera co-signed a loan to pay Aunt Maude's mortgage. Each sister agreed to pay half. Aunt Vera paid half of the first payment and then stopped. She and her family had moved to the suburbs by this time; Aunt Vera said she had to pay her own bills. Aunt Vera and Uncle Bill were both working. Mama, who was supporting a child on one income, was forced to pay all of the remaining payments so her credit rating would not be damaged.

Because of this extra debt, at one point my mother didn't have enough money to pay her half of my tuition. Mama had to work for free for Mrs. Cahan in exchange for a loan to pay my tuition.

There are two main routes to becoming part of that ancient institution—slavery—which derives its name from the Slavs of Eastern Europe. One route is to be captured as a prisoner of war and being forced to work for one's captors. The other even more painful route is to become indebted to a creditor and agreeing to work for that person for free to pay off the debt. Mama's absorption into her sister's financial affairs had resulted in her temporary enslavement.

Mr. Portmann calmed me down. I dried my eyes and went on to math class. He called my mother to tell her what had happened. When I got home, Mama assured me that we would always have enough money. This is when my mother swore never to get involved in her extended family's financial problems again.

Except for math, I enjoyed all my subjects. My poor math skills may have been why I was ten before I could tell time. Mama tried to teach me. Everything made sense until 25 of 11. Moving the hands on the bedside clock around the hound's-tooth clock face . . . 10:20, 10:25, 10:30, 25 of 11? Of course, it would've made sense to me if my mother had just called it 10:35 and forgot about 25 of 11. But Mama had no patience for teaching. Even a *How-To-Tell-Time* book she bought for me didn't help.

One of Aunt Sally's male friends gave me a silver Timex with a numbered face and a black wristband. By the end of the day, I could tell time. I was so enraptured with my watch that I refused to take it off when I went to bed.

Now I could tell time, but my mathematical abilities were so poor that eighth-grade Algebra was a confusing alphabet soup. My math teacher, Mr. Laser, was impatient. He could only teach the students who easily understood algebra. During the parent-teacher conference, Mama discussed my problems with him.

"Wendy has a lot of strong points. She's a good reader, so she does well in English and History, but she's not good in math. She never has been."

"But she doesn't understand basic concepts, so it's impossible to teach her," Mr. Laser responded.

"I don't have patience, and I know it. I could never teach. But if you call yourself a teacher, you should be able to teach anybody."

My mother didn't tell me what Mr. Laser's answer was, but he stopped making me feel bad about not understanding.

I was originally enrolled in Algebra I again, but since I couldn't stand being a year behind my classmates in math I asked to retake Algebra I in the summer. Starting geometry a month after the first class didn't help me at all.

After doing miserably in geometry, I had a surprisingly wonderful time in my Algebra I summer course. My experience with Mr. Laser had been so bad that I did not even remember having seen the concepts when I met them again. It was as if I had been mentally absent the year before. This time I understood the concepts. For the first time, I realized maybe it wasn't my fault that I was bad in math: same subject, same student, different teacher. Mr. Dims was a wonderful teacher. He was patient and clear.

For my tenth-grade year, I had Algebra II with Mr. Dims again. "Math is cumulative!" he always said. I saw the truth of that statement that year. Because I had Algebra I that summer, while my classmates had had a year of geometry in between, I was sharp from the beginning of the year. It was odd that the system interrupted the two algebras.

My favorite question from the final for Algebra II still makes me smile. On the exam, we were told the amount of time it took for a man to rake leaves by himself. Then we were asked to calculate how much time it would take to rake the leaves when the man's four-year-old son helped him.

The answer I came up with showed that it took longer for the man to finish the yard with the assistance of his four-year-old son. When I finished the problem, the number didn't make sense. More people working on a task always meant it took less time to complete the task.

Then I reread the problem. His four-year-old son was probably jumping in the leaves. That was the kind of "help" a four-year-old son would provide.

Serena, my best friend, thought it wasn't a fair question. Serena had changed her correct answer because it hadn't made sense to her.

For the first time I saw math connected to the real world. That's why I liked the question so much. I actually laughed out loud during a math test. Unbelievable!

Despite our fine history teacher, the teaching of American history at Dalton was inadequate. There was only one sentence about slavery in our American history text: "Slavery was not the cause of the Civil War." This huge knowledge gap created a gross misconception. When one of my friends said, "Slavery could not have been that bad; nobody ran away," I headed straight to the Schomburg—the New York Public Library's branch devoted to the history of the African Diaspora—to prove her wrong. The Schomburg became my second home.

From eighth grade on, every research paper I wrote dealt with some aspect of American slavery. My teacher was amazed that a high school student was allowed to use the library's primary sources. Another history teacher routinely kept a copy of my papers for his files. My guess was that neither of these men, both PhD candidates in American history at Columbia University, was being taught anything about African American history.

And so began my lifelong research into the history of black people in America. It eventually led me to an interest in the history and literature of all outsiders, not only in America, but around the world.

Swirling around in a whirl of extracurricular activities—chorus at school (Faure's "Requiem"), choir at church ("Jesu, Joy of Man's Desiring"), acting class scenes (*The Rose Tattoo*), dancing in the recital (*Soulfinger!*), dancing and singing in musicals (*Anything Goes!*), playing small parts in Shakespeare (a witch in *Macbeth*)—I made sure my academic work did not suffer. Sometimes I was panting to keep up with myself, but I thoroughly enjoyed learning the music, the parts, the steps, and being part of a creative whole.

My mother was very enthusiastic about all of the performing arts, but she particularly liked dancing. Big Ma had felt that dancing was sinful, so Mama had never learned how to dance as a child. Once she became an adult, she probably felt too afraid of making mistakes to try to learn.

Starting at age three, I took tap dancing with Mary Bruce. Mary Bruce was a ballet-trained Chicago dance teacher from a dancing family who switched to tap dance when she saw Lew Leslie's black revue Blackbirds. Lew Leslie was a white producer who produced black revues in the '20s and '30s headlining black artists such as Lena Horne and Bill "Bojangles" Robinson, the tap dancer who taught Shirley Temple how to dance in several movies.

When her sister, Sadie, set up a studio in competition with hers, Ms. Bruce left Chicago for New York. Her dance studio was in a Harlem loft on 125th Street.

Mary Bruce taught us children how to do the Suzie Q while we sang "Put another nickel in the nickelodeon/ All I want is music, music, music!" Our dance group appeared at Carnegie Hall (I turned my back to the audience when

I did my dance) and the Brooklyn Academy of Music. Years later I took modern dance, ballet, jazz, Scottish, African, and ballroom dancing.

The point was not to turn me into a performing artist. My mother just wanted me to have fun, develop poise, be creative, and to deeply understand and appreciate the performing arts because I had, even on a basic level, participated in them. Mama was right. Live theater, dance, and music are still vital to me. I both enjoy and am energized by live performances. And even today dancing to Stevie Wonder, Aretha Franklin, Marvin Gaye, and Gladys Knight and the Pips is part of my exercise routine.

The neighbors supported my mother's encouragement of my education. Our small building of twenty-four families was like a small town. Since my comings and goings were as regular as the patrolman on the beat, Miss Tibble, who lived on the first floor, notified Mama one evening that I had not gone to school that day. My mother thanked Miss Tibble for looking out for me, but told her that I was off from school all that week. Dalton's holidays and the public school holidays didn't usually coincide.

In fact, Daltonians went to school a lot more than their public school counterparts. We were off from school for two weeks in December for winter break, a long weekend in February for what was then Washington's Birthday, a week or two for spring break, Memorial Day, and that was it.

School started around the third week in September and ended by the first week in June, Arch Day. That was the only half-day; it was named for the arch which we would walk under to symbolize moving to the next grade. As we walked under the arch, we sang popular tunes with lyrics that we had made up about the past school year.

Despite my busy schedule, I always had time to read books outside of those assigned for classes. To me, the books we read in school were appetizers on the menu. On my own, I devoured the main courses. After my class read a few of Fitzgerald's stories in seventh grade, I liked them so much I spent the summer reading as many of his novels as I could check out of the library. One Christmas, Mama's friend, Jim, gave me a set of James Baldwin's books, including *The Fire Next Time*.

In high school, I seriously considered becoming a writer. My mother was overjoyed. But Mama told me with sadness in her voice that I couldn't make a living at it. It was then that I decided I would work as a journalist during the day and write fiction at night.

Later, when my mother bought the brownstone, she set up my first writing room. It was one flight down from my attic bedroom (I had chosen that room because, from my reading, I knew that writers always lived in the attic). The writing room was a narrow shoebox lined with books. The bookcases on the right-hand wall were interrupted by a gas fireplace. On a small desk in front of the security gate-covered window sat my typewriter.

At first, it was the manual typewriter that a family friend had bought for me "hot" on the street when I was 12. Later, when I was working at the bank, I bought an electric typewriter and spent a year in that room writing a novel after work.

My mother was also important to my writing in more fundamental ways. When I was much younger, I used to listen to Mama and Cousin Ravena talking. Silently, keeping track on my fingers, I counted the topics they discussed. It was amazing how different the first and last topics were from each other. Then I reviewed how they moved from subject to subject. I didn't know it then, but I was teaching myself how to write dialogue.

Also, just like Big Ma, my mother was a storyteller. Often Mama would tell someone a story about an event that I had witnessed. Telling what had happened, my mother made it a little better in the telling. I saw that Mama wasn't lying, just making the story a little more dramatic; I saw that embellishment added spice to reality. This is how I learned to shape a story.

Class trips to lower Manhattan with my acting class opened up the world of people's theater for me. Did Mama know I was going to see "Dionysus 69"?

Everyone in the audience knew that at some point the cast members were going to disrobe. So when the cast began taking off their clothes, nobody should have been surprised. But some tourists in the audience waited until all the actors were completely nude, gawked for five minutes, then walked out scandalized. All the cast members were bony and it was awfully cold. I felt very sorry for them.

My mother always felt that there was no such word as "can't" when it came to doing anything. I discovered that Dalton agreed with her. My seventh-grade class was told to adapt the book we had read, *Boy Knight of Reims*, into a play. It was a story about building a cathedral in the middle Ages. Since none of us had ever written a play, we didn't know we couldn't do it. So we did it. I had the pleasure of playing the part of Old Basi, the villain. The part was too large for one person, so I shared it with two other students in the class.

We often went to museums and zoos. One exhibit at the Museum of the City of New York that particularly stood out for me depicted the blizzard of 1888 in New York City. Up to five feet of snow fell during the storm. Drifts reached a height of 60 feet, and 200 people died in New York (Brooklyn did not become part of the city until 1898). Frozen utility cables caused such havoc that they were put underground. It was the year Big Ma was born, so it was easy to remember.

The zoo was a smelly adventure. The odor in the primate house was repellent, but I liked the penguins. Falling into the pool, while formally dressed in tuxedos, they were hilarious.

From the time I was three or four years old, I had wanted a piano. I wanted to sing and play along like the people I saw in the movies. For my ninth Christmas, my mother bought me an upright Wurlitzer. It took five years for her to pay off the $800 purchase price on the installment plan.

The "idea" of the piano and the reality were quite different. I never learned to read music fluently, so that was an obstacle. Playing the George M. Cohan songs, which I knew by heart, from the movie *Yankee Doodle Dandy*, was what I wanted to do, not practice scales.

Every Fourth of July I stayed up to see the movie starring James Cagney as George M. Cohan on *The Late Show*. The TV was then in the living room and Mama's bedroom was right next to it. Singing the songs (Give my regards to Brooadway/ Remember me to Herald Square . . .) and following the dance numbers as best I could, I had a glorious time. As it grew later, my mother would call for me to go to bed. Finally, about one o'clock, always at the same scene in the movie, she would demand loudly: "Wendy! Go . . . to . . . bed!" That last sentence was said with lots of space between each word, so I knew she meant it.

One year I explained this to Mama and promised if I could just see the whole movie once, I would never stay up to see it again. My mother agreed.

Music theory turned music into math, so that was painful. Once my fingers memorized a piece, I could focus on interpretation, but I could never look up and find my place because my music reading was so poor.

Because the piano had been so expensive, I felt awful. Mama loved music and sometimes would say she wished I could play a song that she liked on the piano. Now I wished my mother had rented a piano so if it hadn't worked out, the piano could have been returned.

Cooking, of course, was also an important part of my education. I don't remember not being in the kitchen with Mama. When I was about four years old I made miniature biscuits to put in the pan alongside my mother's regular-sized ones for Sunday breakfast. At the age of six, I helped my mother by lining up the ingredients on the table, mixing, chopping, and washing the dishes. Once I made a terrible mistake. I started washing a bowl that was full of cream for Mama's floating island dessert. My mother angrily expelled me from the kitchen. Crying, I ran to the couch in the living room. Eventually, I was allowed to return.

By the time I was nine, I considered myself an old hand at cooking. I could follow a recipe, as long as I understood the terms being used. In addition, I knew how to improvise based on what I knew about the different ingredients and how they worked together in a particular dish. At 12, I majored in omelets, cooking my way through Mama's blue McCall's cookbook. Finally I graduated to the Spanish omelet, which was similar to a soufflé cooked in the oven.

My crowning culinary achievement was the steamy day I made beef Stroganoff for my mother's birthday. Looking back, I should have cooked something less stove-intensive on a hot day. We often had salads for dinner in the summer: scoops of tuna fish—mixed with mustard and cardamom, no mayonnaise—eaten out of a bowl made of half a peeled cantaloupe, washed down with homemade lemonade. I couldn't make food beautiful as Mama did, but I certainly knew basic cooking.

In keeping with my mother's practice of giving me more responsibility as I grew older, that same year that I made Spanish omelets was also the year I became solely responsible for the grocery shopping. The two of us would make the list. Then, giving me $100, Mama would say "Here's an extra dollar. If you see something and you don't know what it is, buy a dollar's worth. Come back with it and I'll show you how to eat it." I would take the number 4 bus over to Daitch-Shopwell near Columbia. We didn't do major shopping in Harlem because there was more variety at cheaper prices and better-quality food across 110th Street. After I finished shopping, I would return on the bus with the perishables and have the rest delivered. That was my weekly routine until I graduated from high school.

That is how I discovered fresh artichokes. When I brought them back, my mother steamed them, then made a dipping sauce of melted butter. We dipped the gray-green leaves into the butter and ate them one by one.

Life was going well at Dalton, too. I had found a circle of friends in seventh grade when a large influx of public school students entered middle school. We laughingly called ourselves the "out group." We were black, white, and Latino. They were future artists, writers, scientists, healthcare practitioners, therapists, entrepreneurs, lawyers, and judges.

One year my friends and I arranged a picnic in Clove Lakes Park in Staten Island. But most of the time we spent at Teresa's house; she lived near the school. In her spacious bedroom we discussed our various life philosophies.

When we were hungry, we would raid Teresa's refrigerator. Teresa warned us to be careful because Teresa's mother kept her urine in there for her doctor's appointments. Our group would stay until Teresa's mother took her quietly aside and asked Teresa to ask us to go home. (What her mother actually said was, "Tell those damn kids to get out of here now!" Teresa was supposed to clean it up when she relayed the message to us. As a joke, she did not.)

A year later, we had an impromptu sleepover at my house. During spring break, all of us had been aimlessly wandering around the city. Someone suggested that we go to my house. After finally getting taxis that would take this mélange of black, white, and Latino teenagers to Harlem, we arrived. We were all having such a good time talking that night had fallen before we realized it.

My mother returned from making and serving the Passover seder at the Cahan's apartment. Although she had had a long day and might have been anxious to come home and relax, Mama warmly greeted my friends and immediately told them to call their parents for permission to spend the night.

We ate the leftovers from the Passover seder and camped out on the living room carpet with blankets and pillows. After a few jokes about mice in the walls, we settled down to sleep.

Awakening to the sounds of birds chirping in the morning, we roused ourselves. I walked my classmates to the bus stop. After they left, my mother told me that she had been afraid for them in the neighborhood at night and thought it was too dangerous for them to go home then.

Despite her emphasis on being polite and kind, Mama also taught me to stand up for people when I saw they were being mistreated. This is an incident that I don't completely remember, but when I heard my mother tell it, I could look back and see it in my mind.

From the evidence of Mrs. Cahan's later behavior, it had lasting results.

One of the three jobs that helped Mama pay my tuition came from making the food for weekend parties at Mr. and Mrs. Cahan's summer home. This included a Saturday of drinks, hors d'oeuvres, and dinner for around ten people; my mother would stay overnight and return home on Sunday afternoon. Sometimes I stayed with Aunt Ravena, but often I went with Mama. We would catch the train to Stamford, Connecticut, early on Saturday morning at the 125th Street train station. Either Mr. or Mrs. Cahan would pick us up at the station and drive us to their home in upstate New York. One year, the beautiful little hill above the house, where I tried to pet the scampering rabbits, had been replaced by a swimming pool.

Friends and family members were lounging on beach chairs around the pool. The ice bucket and bottles of seltzer and liquor had already been set up. Mr. Cahan always welcomed me to join the guests. I must have been around four. Watching my mother trudging up the hill from the house with a tray of hors d'oeuvres, I must have thought, "This is not right."

Turning to Mrs. Cahan, I said, "Why don't you get the trays? My mama's tired. She works all wcck."

Mr. Cahan agreed. "Yes, I think you're right, Wendy. Jo shouldn't have to do that. We've got lots of people here who can go down and bring the trays up."

From that time on, whenever we went to the house in the country, a family member would come down to see if the trays were ready to bring up the hill so Mama could concentrate on getting dinner ready.

My friends honored the relationship Mama and I had. One afternoon after school I was with two of my friends, Daniel and Robert, in Carl Schurz Park; I wanted to stay longer. I called home for permission, but my mother said no. I was giving Mama a hard time when Daniel said, "Listen to your mother. At least she cares where you are." I went home.

I kept in touch with several of my friends from that time. Decades later, when I was at Daniel's wedding, I saw him lighting up a cigarette.

"Daniel, I didn't know you smoked. When did you start?"

"I've been smoking since eighth grade," Daniel replied, as he exhaled.

"How come I never saw you smoking?"

"Robert and I both smoked, but we never smoked in front of you because we didn't want to be bad influences. We didn't want to upset your mother."

I had some good friends.

In 1969, at the end of sophomore year, I went with Mama to see the guidance counselor to discuss applying for college. Mr. Rollins, who had formerly been the swimming coach, told us that I should only apply to colleges in the South, since those were the only schools I could get into. I had a solid B average, was ranked 23 in a class of about 95, and had taken French and German.

Later that year I earned 707 on my verbal SAT. This was before the scoring system was changed; it would be closer to 750 on the current scale. As usual, I had scored abysmally low on the math section. I had most of the conventional academic strengths colleges wanted in their students as well as my involvement in the arts and a year volunteering as a candy striper at Metropolitan Hospital with my church's youth group.

"I am the product of an inferior education in the South. Wendy's not going to be another one. I have worked too hard. She can go anywhere she wants to go, but I'm not paying for her to go to any school below the

Mason-Dixon Line," my mother said angrily before we walked out the door.

I bought *Barron's Guide to Colleges* and became my own guidance counselor. After doing the research, I applied to the University of Chicago, Bryn Mawr, Swarthmore, Hampshire, Cornell, and Notre Dame (not the famous one).

"Could you apply to Yale, too?"

"I don't want to go there. It's probably full of a lot of stuck-up people."

"You don't have to go; I just want to see if you can get in. Go where you want, just apply."

So I applied to Yale, determined not to go there. I made Yale my first interview on September 1 of my senior year so I could get it out of the way. Walking into the interview at the admissions office, I expected to see an old gentleman with muttonchop whiskers. Instead, I found a slim, brown-haired man somewhere in his late twenties, around the age of my older male cousins.

We spent the interview talking about Somerset Maugham and the Junior Year Abroad program. I knew I wanted to see other countries and liked the idea of a combination of studying and traveling. The admissions officer suggested I eat lunch at the Kline Biology Tower so I could get a good view of the campus. He also told me about the student tours. I walked around and talked to some of the students already on campus. I was pleasantly surprised to find that I had actually enjoyed Yale, but was interested in seeing other schools before making up my mind.

I was also surprised to see a modern sculpture on campus called *Lipstick (Ascending) on Caterpillar Tracks*, created by Claes Oldenburg. The name describes it well. Students had spray-painted the sculpture with anti-Vietnam War graffiti and phallic jokes. I thought it was wonderful that the administration allowed the students to express themselves so freely.

By the beginning of senior year, my top choices were the University of Chicago, Yale, Cornell, and Swarthmore. The University of Chicago had arranged an interview in New York at a restaurant with an alumna. The two of us had a fine rapport. I was ready to pack my bags that night. In the spring, the university arranged for free tickets and overnights in the dorms for students who could not afford to make the trip on their own. Tours, lunch, and meetings with freshmen were all arranged.

My mother and I had matching clipboards with information about the trip. In an *I Love Lucy*-inspired mix-up, I ended up with the parent's information and documents and Mama ended up with the student's information and documents. I had to get all my documents reissued after I arrived at the university.

The weather added to the complications. On April 1 it snowed. That was it. I refused to go to a college where it snowed the first day of April. Of course, it was also going to be too expensive to come home for Thanksgiving or the occasional weekend if I wanted to. At the time, I wasn't able to admit to myself that I wanted to live away from home, but not that far away.

The choice was now narrowed down to Yale, Swarthmore, and Cornell. At Cornell I met a group of black students who wanted to tell me what to say, what to do, and what to wear to be considered black. I wanted none of that.

In the end, the guidance counselor was wrong. I was accepted everywhere I applied. The University of Chicago gave me the most financial aid, so I told my mother I would go there.

"Where do you want to go? Don't worry about the money."

"I want to go to Yale."

"When I was growing up I told myself that if I had a child, I would want that child to go to Yale, and here you are going."

My mother waited until I had made my decision before telling me about her lifelong dream. I felt no pressure to choose to go there. How did Mama, as a black girl growing up in the rural South in the '20s and '30s, envision a child she did not have going to a college that was not only Ivy League, but for most of its history mostly white Anglo-Saxon Protestant male? My mother's vision and her imagination had no bounds. In total, five seniors from Dalton ended up going to Yale. Three of us were friends from what we jokingly called the "out group."

YALE UNIVERSITY

Although my admission to Yale University ended the daily presence of my mother in my educational life, a great deal of what I did there and how I reacted to what I found there had to do with her. I was on my own, and gladly so. But even at Yale, she was still nurturing my education.

When I arrived on campus, I saw that the Lipstick sculpture had been removed. Despite my disappointment, I decided to stay. (Although both the Yale University Visitor Center website and the *Oldenburgvanbruggen* website report the sculpture was removed from March 1970 until October 1974, I saw it in the fall of 1970.)

In addition to the money my mother had saved, that first year I had the National Merit Scholarship and some financial aid. Tuition and room and board my first year at Yale was $5,000.

Every summer I put all my money toward college expenses. Over four years, I paid about 25 percent of my total tuition with my summer earnings. I paid for books, and other on-campus expenses, with the salary from my work-study job as a research assistant for the Frederick Douglass Papers, headed by the late Professor John Blassingame of the African American Studies Department. My share of my father's Social Security also went to college tuition. When I graduated, I was the only person I knew in my income bracket with no student loan debt. This was, in large part, due to Mama.

I became a Literature major. It was different from the English major, because it could be custom-designed. The Literature major allowed me to combine literature from all over the world with any other subject area. My choice was African American and American Indian history, I wanted to continue the delightful task of finding out more about my heritage.

The work at Yale was no more difficult than what I had had at Dalton; there was just more of it, along with more distractions. At Dalton, an extracurricular activity such as rehearsing for the school play could not last longer than 5:30 during the week. In contrast, at Yale, rehearsals could last until midnight. For that reason, I did not try out for any plays.

I was intoxicated with what I was learning. Professor Maria Luisa Nuñes discussed the differences between the original Portuguese and the translations of Brazilian literature we were reading. I discovered in the late Professor Tönu Parming's class that decision making often meant moving ahead with incomplete information. Professor Blassingame's teaching assistant, then known as Julie Jones, brought the African American history material to life by having students teach some of the small group seminars.

During my sophomore year, I buried myself in my work. One semester, with special permission, I took seven courses so I wouldn't have time to talk to anybody. That semester I took an intensive Spanish course; the class was held eight days a week. Saturday classes had two sessions, so students joked that was the eighth day. I benefited from the team of teachers, each with slightly different accents, headed by Professor Margie Resnick.

And then there was social life. I was fortunate to have suitemates, a roommate, and next-door neighbors, who were congenial. But my roommate, with whom I could easily have become close friends, spent all her time outside of classes with her boyfriend. It was difficult for someone not living on Old Campus, where most of the first-year students lived, to make female friends. Because I didn't have a close girlfriend to discuss relationships with, I made a royal mess of my romantic life.

After nine years at Dalton, I had been anxious to dive into the adventurous world of college at Yale University. I expected scintillating conversations and students who valued and applauded people who were different.

Like my mother, I was an outsider in my extended family. My cousins had mixed feelings toward me. They were proud of my intelligence and looked up to me as a role model while at the same time they made fun of me for going to a "white" school; so I was especially anxious to meet black people who enjoyed learning and were proud of it.

Instead, I found some middle-class black males copying the diction and style of a popular black movie hero of the time: a pimp nicknamed Super Fly. But when they spoke to white women, they sounded like British professors. Most of these young men had either attended private schools as I had or had gone to superb public schools such as Bronx High School of Science.

Many of the white students seemed to believe that black students were admitted to Yale to fulfill racial quotas, but were not as intelligent as their white counterparts. A black Yalie, who was in one of my first-year English classes, told me that he had overheard his white roommate talking about me to another classmate. The white student was amazed that I had used a word in class discussion which he didn't know.

I was also shocked at some of the outrageous behavior of my fellow white Yalies. One evening at dinner, several white male students had a food fight. Throwing food around, they acted like unsupervised two-year-olds. Afterwards, the dining room staff cleaned up the mess.

I was sure that none of these white males came from public schools or were the first in their families to go to college. These students were most likely privileged males who had gone to prep schools and had come from wealthy families. I wished Mama could have taken the place of one of these arrogant students.

In January of my sophomore year, I met a new black female student, Zora Robinson. She had started with the class a year ahead of mine. However, Zora had been so upset by the students she met that she felt compelled to take a year off. Her passion for filmmaking was attacked by other black Yalies: "Black people are not interested in making movies! That's for white people." Now she was in my class.

"I thought that Yale would be like Córdoba in Spain," said Zora as she paused and made a deadpan expression. "I was mistaken."

I started laughing and never stopped.

In addition to the Super Fly imitators, some of the black men were pseudo-black nationalists speaking in the rhythms of the black Baptist preacher: "The black woman has castrated the black man. She has to walk behind him so the brother can lead."

One evening in the main dining hall, Zora and I had a major argument with these men. We told our fellow black Yalies that we knew they had black mothers and grandmothers who had sacrificed so they could attend Yale. The brothers should not be disrespecting these black women. Zora and I added that we were not walking behind anybody. From the corners of my eyes, I could see the supportive smiles of the black female dining hall staff. I knew Mama would have been cheering me on too if she had been there.

The concept of the "black matriarchy" was in the air at the time both from militant black leaders and white policymakers. Malcolm X—until his break with the Black Muslims—adhered to the belief that black women should be limited to bearing children and cooking food. His ideas on women, as did his ideas on race, evolved after he was forced from his position as minister of Temple No. 7 in Harlem. In the Organization of Afro-American Unity, one of the two groups that X founded after leaving the Black Muslims, black women held leadership positions.

On the white policymaker side, Patrick Moynihan, Assistant Secretary of Labor under Johnson, who had a doctorate in sociology with a specialty in ethnic studies, had written in 1965 "The Negro Family: The Case for National Action," popularly known as the "Moynihan Report." According to Moynihan, the "problem" of black female-headed households was at the center of the destruction of the black family. Only years later did Moynihan report that the jobs that black working-class men were allowed to have could not support a spouse and two children.

Moynihan himself came from a broken home. I don't like this pejorative term, but that is what a single-parent home was called at the time. One day he was living in Nassau County, Long Island, during the school year and enjoying summers in Bluffton, Indiana, with his grandfather, and the next he was shining shoes in Times Square to buy milk for the family. In 1937, Moynihan's father, amid whispers of "another woman," left Moynihan's mother and their three children. Moynihan, at ten, was the oldest. He never saw his father again. The family never regained financial stability.

My emotional experience at Yale changed for the better because of my friendship with Zora. She was bright and witty and attracted a group of writers, actors, musicians, and other creative souls around her. These students were black, white, mixed-race, Chicana, gay, straight, and undecided; in other words, the college version of my Dalton friends. From then on, I felt right at home.

Some of my friends produced an undergraduate production of *To Be Young, Gifted, and Black* that was presented in the subscription series at the Long Wharf Theater.

Although I couldn't jeopardize my studies by trying out for a play, I continued my involvement with the arts that Mama had initiated. Zora, Dennis (known as the "laughing cameraman" because his laughter could be heard on the soundtrack), and I created a documentary called *The Ebony Belles Present the Easter Egg Hunt* for our film class. It depicted a neighborhood Easter egg hunt given by black women who had founded a New Haven community group.

In my junior year, my short story, *Lily*, won second place in the Wallace Fiction Writing Contest, which was named in honor of the son of broadcast journalist Mike Wallace. Wallace's son had wanted to be a writer, but had died in a climbing accident.

I worked on the story with David Milch, the television writer known for *NYPD Blue* and *Deadwood,* as part of his literature class. The respect that Mr. Milch showed my work as I revised the story removed any small doubts I had that I could become a writer.

Students, even people I didn't know, who read the first-place winner, published in the *Yale Daily News*, asked to read my story and felt it should've won first place. That success encouraged me to apply to the Scholar of the House Program in my senior year.

The Scholar of the House was Yale's independent study program. There were twelve scholars, one for each residential college. Each of us worked on a project with the guidance of an advisor with whom we met at least weekly. Once a week, the scholars and administrators of the program also gathered for dinner. Taking turns, we gave presentations on our projects to the group. I wrote a novel, *Shorty.* Others shot movies, wrote research papers, or created paintings. I completed the novel ahead of schedule. It was accepted by the professors who interviewed me in fulfillment of my work for senior year.

My main character was based on the family friend who had given me the typewriter on which I was writing the novel. But I didn't know enough about my character's world—he was a number runner—to write from his point of view, so the novel was weak. But the experience of waking up every morning confronting an empty page and spending day and night making sure that the story progressed was a good one for me. I was confident I had found my life's work. Now I had to find a way to support myself while I did it.

One incident marred that scintillating year of creativity. Yale has a college system, based on the Oxford University system. What at other colleges are called dorms are called residential colleges at Yale. And they are more than dorms. There were twelve of them at that time; there are fourteen now, each with a distinctive name, history, and culture. Each college has its own dining hall and classrooms for seminars. Some have theaters for plays, others have areas for sports, and most have a weekly newsletter. Each college creates a microcosm of the larger university. I lived in Davenport College my last two years at Yale.

Even when I wasn't writing, I was living the story in my head, so I walked around campus in a trance. In my usual fog, one evening I wandered down to the dining room for the meeting about the next year's room placements.

In the past, room placement had been conducted using the lottery system. The juniors were the first to choose their rooms for senior year. Each group of students selected one person from their group of suitemates to select a number from a box. Those with the highest numbers were allowed the first choice of rooms in the available pool of rooms. The sophomores, the next year's juniors, followed and chose their rooms.

Finally, the freshmen, the next year's sophomores, had their pick of the rooms that were left. The incoming freshmen were placed by the university since they, of course, were not yet on campus. The student-run room draw committee had called this meeting to get suggestions for other ways to select rooms.

My suitemates and I were graduating, so the room draw wouldn't affect us. But we thought it would be nice to show the winners of our suite where they would be living next year. There were five of us in all.

We lived in a small building that was surrounded by the larger building and gates of Davenport College, but had its own set of stairs and entrance. It was called "the cottage." Although we shared a common room and a bathroom, we each had our own bedroom.

I was only half listening as students batted around ideas. Then I thought I heard a white male Yalie say, "I don't like the way the system is now. If you get a low number, it's like being a nigger in the South."

How could he possibly compare getting beaten, castrated, lynched, and burned in the South to getting a bad room in the Yale room draw? Wasn't this like saying waiting in a long line in the grocery store was like waiting in a long line at Auschwitz? How could he trivialize black people's suffering like that? And why did he think he could so casually use that word?

The meeting continued as people made suggestions. I thought, *He couldn't have said that, because somebody would've said something.*

When the meeting broke up without a final decision as to how to conduct the room draw, I returned to the cottage with my suitemates. They assured me that I had heard correctly. A black male Yale senior from another residential college said he wasn't surprised. The student was an ignorant person, and we should just ignore him.

"Don't you think we should do something?" I asked.

"What can we do?" one of my suitemates asked.

"I'm just concentrating on getting out of here," said the visiting senior.

I decided to talk to the Master of Davenport College. "Master" was the title of the administrator who ran the residential college. Even though I knew it had its roots in the British use of the word meaning teacher, I hated the term. It reminded me of slavery.

Because of my years-long immersion in the history of American slavery, for me, it happened yesterday. Slavery was as close as my grandmother's touch. Born in 1888,

Big Ma had been touched by the formerly enslaved and she, in turn, had touched me.

The head of Davenport was disturbed by what the student had said. She told me that she, too, as a Jewish woman in the college, had been discriminated against. She suggested I write something in the weekly student-run college newsletter.

I wrote a milquetoast paragraph for the newsletter. Recounting what the student had said, I stated that some black students had been upset. I asked the person to be more careful in the future. The staff assured me that the paragraph would appear in the next newsletter.

When the newsletter came out, what I wrote was not in it. Now I understood why some black people felt it necessary to burn down buildings instead of going through channels when they were offended. Finally, I bumped into the administrator.

"Oh, Wendy, I've been looking all over for you. I decided that the newsletter shouldn't print what you wrote because some people might get their feelings hurt."

I walked away. Clearly, black people's feelings didn't matter. Either that or the administrator did not consider black students people. I had expected more from her. When I told my suitemates what had happened, they were not surprised.

Sometime later, the white male juniors who had won the room draw knocked on our door and we gave them a tour of the cottage.

This wasn't the only incident of this kind. In that same week, there were two others. The more egregious of the two occurred when Leonora, a black female student, was applying for a grant for an undergraduate research project. She wanted to go to Haiti. After Leonora finished her presentation and was on her way out, she passed the young white male student who was coming in. Leonora heard one of the white male Yale professors say as this student walked in, "And now we have one of our own."

Yale was an institution in a racist culture. Why did I expect it to be better than the culture that it was part of? I was naïve.

Because of the wonderful time I was having with Zora and my other friends, I had decided to stay at Yale my junior year instead of taking a junior year abroad. With the Yale-in-China Program, I would have another chance to travel.

This program was started in 1901 to foster understanding between the West and China. It was specifically for people who knew nothing about China.

Students would spend two years teaching and living in China. At my interview, I had the pleasure of meeting and speaking with Rev. Sloane Coffin, one of the first well-known clergymen to protest against the Vietnam War and one of several religious leaders active in the civil rights movement.

I ended up as the first alternate in case the person who had been chosen for the program was unable to go. This had nothing to do with racism. A poor interview was the culprit here.

For my graduation present, Mama offered me a six-week all-expenses-paid trip to Europe. Because I felt Mama had sacrificed enough for my education, I refused her offer. I felt it was up to me to fund my own travel. Besides, I wanted to shop in the markets, complain about the bus being late—again—and live day to day in the country.

WORKING IN TOKYO

The *Invest Yourself!* Program at Riverside Church in Manhattan was just what I was looking for. The church had a long history of social activism. Martin Luther King Jr. had given his first speech against the Vietnam War on April 4, 1967, a year to the day before he was assassinated, at Riverside Church. The booklet described opportunities to live and work in communities all over the world for anyone with a college degree. All paid a nominal living stipend, but the true enrichment was the experience.

In September of 1975, I went to Tokyo to teach English as a Second Language to high school students at Toyo Eiwa Jogakuin, a girl's private school established by Canadian Methodists in 1884, which educated students from kindergarten through university. I had a two-year contract. The qualities that my mother had encouraged helped me to live and work successfully in Japan.

In Japan, I was frequently praised by the Japanese people I met because I used chopsticks well and was willing to try any food put before me. I ate sushi, all kinds of soba (noodles); I even ate seaweed, soy sauce, and raw egg with rice in the morning for breakfast. One of my favorite dishes was unagi (cooked eel).

After I had been gone a year, my mother started feeling uncharacteristically exhausted. Mama went to her doctor to find out what was wrong. All her test results were normal. Her doctor told my mother he could find nothing wrong with her. Then he asked, as usual, how I was and what I was doing. My mother told him that I was living and working in Japan. The doctor said, "There's your answer. You're missing her. I'm not going to write a prescription for you for medicine you don't need. Go see Wendy."

Mama took all of her vacation at once and visited me for six weeks in April, just in time for the cherry blossoms. My mother came to my classes, answered questions, and showed her portfolio of culinary art. One of my students invited us to her home for dinner so Mama could show my student's mother how to transform an apple into a swan-like bird with a straight knife.

This was a rare treat. In Japan most socializing with foreigners is Japanese businessmen inviting foreign businessmen to lunch or dinner in a restaurant. Everyone my mother met marveled at how young she looked.

While I went back to work, Mama traveled with my friend, Noriko, to her birthplace, Hiroshima. But if Noriko's grandmother had gone to the market on the morning of August 6, 1945, as she had intended, my friend would have never been born. My class of patent attorneys, whom I taught one evening a week, also invited us to dinner, this time at a tatami (Japanese-style) restaurant. During my vacation, I took my mother to Kyoto, where we stayed in a Japanese inn and visited temples. Mama had a fine time and marveled that I was able to ask for directions and understand them so we could get on the right trains.

While living in Japan, I visited Malaysia, Indonesia, Korea, and the Philippines. Muhammad Ali had recently had a fight in Malaysia. When I walked through the streets with my white fellow teachers, the Indians in the street looked at me and gave me the black power salute as they yelled *Muhammad Ali!* One of the Indians told me that the British had enslaved Indians and brought them to Malaysia, so they felt a connection with black people.

The Korean women were very outspoken. During a light rain, my friend, Sarah, and I visited Seoul's Oldtown, a reconstruction of a Korean folk village. I was wearing pants, had a medium-sized afro, no earrings, no makeup, and was wrapped up in a light raincoat. Sarah was tall, thin, had short hair, was also not wearing makeup, and was dressed the same as I was.

The two of us were greeted with cries of "Yeoja molla? Yeoja molla? (YOja MOEla? YOja MOEla?)." It was clearly a question, but we didn't understand what the Korean women were asking us.

We memorized the phrase and repeated it to our missionary hosts, who were fluent in Korean. It took a long time for our hosts to stop laughing. After hauling them out from underneath the couch, we found out what the women had been asking us: "Are you women? We don't know. Are you women? We don't know."

After my two-year term at the school was over, I spent my third year studying the Japanese language at the International Christian University (ICU) during the day and acting on NHK radio's English as a Second Language program, English for Tomorrow, at night. NHK is the Japanese educational channel, similar to PBS in the United States. I had appeared on the television version of the program the year before.

The summer of 1978, when I finished my Japanese course, I gave myself a graduation present of a few weeks backpacking in Hokkaido, the northern island of the archipelago. Although I wasn't fluent, I could understand a great deal and made all my travel arrangements in Japanese.

CIRCLING THE GLOBE

When I left Japan in the fall of 1978, I spent four months circling the globe. Leaving from Yokohama on a ship named after the Russian lake, Baikal, I boarded the Trans-Siberian Railroad, traveling through and stopping in Russia, Poland, Germany, Italy, Greece, Spain, and France. My rudimentary Spanish, French, and German were quite useful. I was even able to use my basic Spanish to be understood in Italy.

I had many enriching encounters with people, history, art, and culture. On the Trans-Siberian Railroad, I spoke with an Austrian who had long planned this trip with his wife. She had died of cancer. He decided to go on the trip anyway, knowing she would have wanted him to.

He had been a prisoner of war in World War II. Even though many of the Austrians did not know what the war was about, Hitler had put them on the front line so they could be killed or captured first. Prisoners were not allowed to smoke, but the black American guards always gave him cigarettes. He was grateful for their kind treatment.

I met my mother in Paris a few days before Christmas. Mama had come to the City of Light that she had wanted to see since 1927, when Lindbergh had made his historic transatlantic flight. Our first Parisian dinner was a perfectly cooked soufflé. It was a fine end to my three years in Japan.

So much of what I had done was a result of the sacrifices of generations of black people who had preceded me and the love and wisdom handed down to me from my family. Big Ma captivated me with family stories which sparked my love of history and storytelling.

When the doctor assisting at Big Ma's labor had asked Big Pa which one he should save, the mother or the baby, Big Pa's love for Big Ma and the baby anxious to be born had made it impossible for him to make a choice. He had replied, "Save them both."

As an adult, my mother treasured the advice her father gave her: "Get an education. They can't take that away from you." This black woman from Cross Hill, South Carolina, who had fought so hard to finish high school, made certain that all kinds of experiences she never had were made available to me.

Although we had different personalities, the two of us saw education and learning of all kinds as an important aspect of the good life. Mama's hopes for success were not just centered on me. I saw my mother encourage everyone she knew to live a life fueled by passion.

After my father left, Mama did not lose hope. She could have drowned in depression, turned to men or alcohol, but, thankfully, she did not. Instead, my mother shared her vision of life with me: despite obstacles, I could use my intelligence and creativity to become whatever I wanted to be.

And for that, I thank her.

NOTES

Prologue

<u>Page xii</u> **My mother was born to Anna Nance and Scott Ebaugh:** The family name went through many spelling changes: Ebo to Ebough to Ebaugh. But the original spelling that Big Pa had grown up with, Ebo, hints at the eighteenth-century spelling of Igbo, the African people originally hailing from present-day Nigeria. It is possible that he was an Igbo; the Igbo were prized by slave traders then for their farming skills. In modern times, the Igbo—now known for their high educational attainment—in the '60s unsuccessfully fought a civil war in Nigeria to create the nation of Biafra.

Chapter 1: Farming with Father

<u>Page 1</u> **At the same time:** Rosalyn Terborg-Penn, *African American Women in the Struggle for the Vote, 1850–1920* (Bloomington: Indiana University Press, 1998), 153.

Page 1 **In 1920, despite active opposition:** Black suffragettes in South Carolina had formed an organization, the South Carolina Women's Rights Association, as early as 1870 to fight for their right to vote. According to historian Benjamin Quarles, as quoted by historian Rosalyn Terborg-Penn in *African American Women in the Struggle for the Vote, 1850–1920*, these African American women did actually vote in South Carolina in 1870 and, "by this act the Negro became the first practical vindicator of women's right to the ballot" (23–24).

When the white suffragette, Virginia B. Young, wrote a history of the movement in South Carolina, she began it with the organization she founded in 1890, the South Carolina Woman Suffrage Association, thus writing the black women out of the history books.

Page 6 **My mother never went:** It was not only pride that compelled my grandfather to ensure that my grandmother not work outside of their home. White men, just as in slavery times, were notorious for sexually harassing or assaulting black women in their employ. Since black men could not testify against white men in court, and the concept of rape, in terms of black women, did not exist, there was no legal recourse.

<u>Page 19</u> **Some of these men left:** Some of these men may have found other women and started new families. But because of Douglas Blackmon's book, *Slavery by Another Name: the Re-Enslavement of Black Americans from the Civil War to World War II* (2009), and the PBS documentary based on the book, we now know that there is another strong possible reason for the disappearance of these men.

Tens of thousands of black men, en route to northern cities to find work to support their families, were captured and sold to "convict" labor camps. Their "crimes," under the catchall vagrancy laws, usually included nothing more than walking to a train or standing on a corner. When the men were unable to pay the court fine, the amount being equal to a week's wages, the judge turned them over to the white man who had paid it. The enslaved spouses, fathers, brothers, and sons (some as young as 14) would then be forced to "work off" the debt in coal mines (for U.S. Steel in Alabama), brickyards, plantations, and railroads. Worked and beaten to death or shot trying to escape, most were never heard from again. Only President Roosevelt's fear in 1941 of enemy propaganda about America's treatment of African Americans ended this twentieth-century slavery.

Chapter 2: Getting an Education

Page 20 **The national standard high school:** James D. Anderson, email message to author, April 14, 2011.

Page 25 **Julius Rosenwald's Foundation was:** In 1930 the Rosenwald Fund surveyed students at Sterling High School (my mother's high school) in Greenville, South Carolina. Although 83 percent of the parents of the students worked in semi-skilled or unskilled jobs, only one student in the survey was interested in following in their parents' footsteps. Despite this, the fund insisted that students be trained for the "Negro jobs," such as janitors, porters, washerwomen, and child nurses available in the community.

Even though black educators and parents were forced to accept a smaller donation from the fund, they refused to have a high school dedicated exclusively to industrial education. Anderson, *The Education of Blacks in the South, 1860–1935,* 224.

Sterling High School's principal successfully fought the state officials to offer French for Mama's last two years of high school. Interview with Josephine E. Jones, Edison, undated.

Page 25 **The average white American:** Through donations of money, labor, and materials, blacks contributed as much as two-thirds of the cost of their schoolhouses. In addition, the school taxes they paid went to the white schools, so they were doubly taxed without representation; cited in James D. Anderson, *The Education of Blacks in the South, 1860–1935* (Chapel Hill: University of North Carolina Press, 1988), 236.

Anderson quotes DuBois as saying that Black Reconstruction politicians were responsible for legislating for free public schools for all citizens of the South. Ibid.19.

> As DuBois demonstrated, "The first great mass movement for public education at the expense of the state, in the South, came from Negroes." Black politicians played a critical role in establishing universal education as a basic right in southern constitutional conventions during congressional Reconstruction. Under the Military Reconstruction Acts passed in 1867, Congress empowered the generals of the armies of occupation to call for new constitutional conventions in which blacks were to participate along with whites. Black politicians and leaders joined with Republicans in southern constitutional conventions to legalize public education in the constitutions of the former Confederate states.

Later, in the 1960s, these same citizens protested attending school with the very people who had made it possible for them to go to those schools in the first place.

Page 38 **I graduated in 1943:** In 1940, 1,881 black people graduated from high school in South Carolina. The number of graduates in 1943 was probably not much more than that. Perhaps it was less, with many leaving to go to the war. (1940 U.S. Census).

Chapter 3: Domestic Work

Page 48 **That's why it's always puzzled me:** The late Senator Ted Kennedy drove his car off a bridge in Chappaquiddick, Massachusetts, in 1969. His passenger, campaign worker Mary Jo Kopechne, died. Sen. Kennedy survived and said that he swam from Chappaquiddick Island to Edgartown. He did not report the accident for ten hours. He later withdrew his presidential bid.

Page 52 **So there I was:** My mother and I were visiting the Cahans one night when Mama spoke about how she first began working for Mrs. Cahan. Mr. Cahan had asked how long my mother had worked for them on and off. It was about 30 years then. He said that what Mrs. Cahan had done was illegal and Mama could have sued her for false representation. Mrs. Cahan laughed guiltily.

Chapter 4: Life with Len

<u>Page 79</u> **Because I didn't want to:** I heard this story for the first time while writing this book. First I was shocked; then I became angry. My mother had told me about my father only after, at four years old, I finally understood, from talking with my cousins, that fathers were not optional. She had told me that the marriage broke up because my father refused to work. My mother had always emphasized my father's good qualities: he could do math in his head, he was a good dancer, and he was the life of the party.

Slowly I realized that Mama hadn't told me about the violence because she didn't want me to hate my father. My mother said that my sense of humor and love of dancing came from my father.

<u>Page 87</u> **Mr. Cahan filled out:** Mama couldn't get a divorce in New York City because she didn't have enough money to "prove" adultery. She would've had to hire a phony "other woman" and a detective to take a picture of this other woman in a hotel room with Len. This minor industry developed to document adultery, the only legal grounds for divorce at that time, in a way that would hold up in court. A legal separation would also protect her from responsibility for Len's debts.

Recently, I asked Mama how she felt when Len's brother asked her if she wanted to visit Len in the hospital.

My mother said, as if it were wrenched out of her heart, "I wanted to see him; I loved him! He was a nice guy. He just wouldn't work." As the years passed, his abuse was no longer foremost in her memory.

Mama had been going to see Len in the hospital for a few weeks without telling me. Seeing that he was near death, she asked me if I wanted to see him. I didn't remember meeting my father when I was four. So I decided, after some hesitation, to go because this would probably be the last time I would see him. The day I went to see him was June 14, his birthday, Father's Day, and the day I later found out that he met my mother. I was 13. He died on July 2.

Chapter 5: Family Burdens

<u>Page 104</u> **Now I had to try:** My mother's youngest brother was called CJ until he went into the Army. She gave him the name Calvin James to go with the initials so he would have something to put down on the application. When Calvin was nine, Mama's brother-in-law, her oldest sister's husband, a grown man, made Calvin drunk as a joke. Big Pa beat Calvin, but my mother stood up for him. She said it was her brother-in-law who should have been beaten. An alcoholic and heavy smoker all his adult life,

Calvin stopped drinking and smoking cold turkey when he was 80. He died two years later.

Calvin lived with us several times while I was growing up. My first memory of Calvin is of him taking me to Central Park when I was four. We walked and bounced a ball back and forth. We played so long I got tired. Calvin carried me back home in his arms. He told me I was heavy and grumbled good-naturedly that he wasn't going to take me to the park again if I couldn't walk back.

Page 110 **Like Vera, Bill, Nina and Nelson:** In 1961, Vera and her family of four were evicted from their apartment. The notices that the city was demolishing the building on 145th Street where they lived had been given to them the year before. It was a federal program to replace the projects. Each family was offered $10,000 to move before a certain date. Aunt Vera refused to move. After the date passed, the family was forced to leave that summer "with nothing but the clothes on their backs," a phrase from Aunt Vera's letter which Big Ma walked around ominously repeating as she mournfully shook her head while I was down there that summer.

The family stayed with us for a year. Except for dropping me off at school, which allowed Mama to stop paying my caretaker extra to do so, Aunt Vera and her family did not contribute anything to the household.

After that, they moved to a house in the suburbs and made snide comments about people who lived in Harlem.

Page 110 "**Let me take care of all:** Despite the many problems, when I was very young I saw only the good times with my extended family. When I went down south to see Big Ma in June, I got off the train, rode the car to my grandmother's house, took off my shoes, and didn't put them on again until it was time to go back to New York in September. I picked blackberries off the bushes near the railroad tracks and golden-green scuffodines, a type of grape, off the tree next to the front porch.

The house stood on brick legs to protect it from flooding. I made mud pies under the house. The summer my cousins had a dog, I baked mud pies in the sun and offered a few to him. Blackie licked them gratefully. Perched in a small tree—I couldn't climb the larger ones—I wrote letters to Mama about the fun I was having.

My relatives' friends were my friends. Once I became upset about something and was determined to take the train back to New York. Without money or luggage, I began walking to the nearby station. When I passed Miss Gussie's house, she asked me where I was going. Somehow I ended up stopping to play with Miss Gussie's children and forgot all about going back to New

York. Everywhere I went, I had a new last name: I wasn't Wendy Jones; everyone called me Wendy, Jo's daughter.

On the Fourth of July, I ran two houses down to my oldest aunt's house where my grown cousin was having a barbecue. Taking the chili dog my cousin offered, I tried not to spill the sloppy dog on my blouse and shorts as I bit into its juicy spiciness.

I enjoyed seeing Ken, Ben, and Steve, Aunt Vera's children. Ken and Ben, seven years older than me, were fraternal twins. Their brother, Steve, was two years younger than they were.

Most of the time they wouldn't play with me because I was a girl. But sometimes they would play Red Devil. Standing in the yard in front of Big Ma's front porch steps, Steve was the scary devil. The devil would come asking for various fruits and vegetables. If Steve named the one I had chosen, I had to run all the way to my aunt's yard and around the dogwood tree and back into my grandmother's yard without being tagged. Steve was thin and quite fast. I laughed and screamed as he tagged me. Now, I was out.

Ken and Ben did not look that much alike. Ken was normal weight and pecan-brown with a round face. Ben had an oval-shaped face with sharp features. He was slim with a fine sheen to his rich, dark brown, blackstrap-molasses skin: he resembled the Black Indian mix of Big Ma's side of the family.

Ken, who was not very talkative, drove adults crazy. Someone in authority would lay down the law to Ken. He would nod politely and not talk back. Then Ken would go off and do the opposite of whatever the adult thought he had agreed to.

One day I hitched a ride on the handlebars of Ken's bicycle. As we were slowing down for a red light, the front wheel of the bicycle rolled over a partially straightened wire hanger. The curve of the hanger was heading straight toward my right eye. Ken saw it and leaned to the left so we would fall over. He made me promise not to tell the adults how close I had come to getting seriously hurt.

Ben taught me how to aim and shoot a slingshot. I didn't expect much success, because he said I wasn't doing it right. When Ben left, I aimed the rock-loaded slingshot at a truck passing on the street in front of my grandmother's house. Bull's-eye! I hit the truck driver's side window and cracked it. An angry truck driver came storming out of his truck and down the inclined path into the yard to talk to Big Ma. I don't remember what happened next, but I never would have aimed at the truck if I had known I was going to hit it.

My grandmother played her favorite trick on me. I was one of the youngest grandchildren, so I didn't know it was an old trick. Like all the other grandchildren, I was captivated by Big Ma's pipe. I had never seen a woman smoke a pipe. My grandmother usually smoked it in the afternoons while sitting in the red and white aluminum chair on the front porch. Big Ma said she started smoking after Big Pa died to calm her nerves, and it helped her remember him. I didn't understand what the smoking had to do with it, because Mama had told me that Big Pa didn't smoke.

Anyway, my grandmother asked me to bring her the red, white and blue pouch with her George Washington tobacco in it so she could fill her pipe. Once Big Ma had the pipe going, I asked her if I could take a puff.

"Sure, baby."

I took the pipe and inhaled as I had seen people do with cigarettes. Coughing and nearly choking, I quickly handed the pipe back.

Her shoulder-length mixed-gray braids glinted silver in the sunlight as my grandmother laughingly said, "You don't smoke a pipe like that, baby!"

I was through with the pipe-smoking experiment.

Big Ma wasn't always playing practical jokes. Sometimes we pored over old photo albums. Big Ma showed me pictures of my second cousin's eldest daughter. I struggled to understand how these people were related to me. Even this white man with straight hair and what appeared to be blue eyes in the black-and-white wall-sized framed picture was a family member. His name was Isaiah Jordan, my grandmother's grandfather. Big Ma said that he married an Indian who was Big Ma's grandmother. Their daughter was Emma Jordan, who, when she married George Nance, became Emma Nance, Big Ma's mother.

Often we were partners in secrecy making supper. If a string bean or a potato fell on the floor, Big Ma washed it off, put it back in the pot, and asked me not to tell my cousins. If I did, they would say it would give them cooties and refuse to eat it.

Later, I began to see things I didn't like about my extended family. Those houses in Greenville where Big Ma, my aunts, uncles, and cousins lived and where I had my Huck Finn summers? They had a complicated history.

Originally, Mama had planned to buy three houses adjoining each other on a parcel of land that resembled a long oblong-shaped bowl, or valley. This was colored property about a mile from the railroad tracks. It may have been undesirable for white buyers because the sight and sound of the railroad was omnipresent, but as a child I loved the sound of the train whistle, both lonesome and adventurous, as it departed going north to New York or on the return trip going further south to New Orleans.

My mother intended one of the houses for Aunt Clara, the aunt she had stayed with when she went to high school; one was for Big Ma, and the third one was to provide rental income for the two elderly women. Mama had saved the down payment money from her wages for Big Ma's part of the property. Aunt Clara had given my mother the money she had saved from taking in laundry for the down payment on her part of the property. Mama had to work, so she couldn't attend the closing. So she sent down a signed blank check from New York for her oldest sister to give to the seller to represent Aunt Clara and Big Ma, who were to be co-owners.

When the closing was over, my mother's oldest sister and her spouse, through a stratagem I was never able to understand, were listed on the deed as co-owners with Big Ma when not a dime of the money belonged to them. The older sister and her spouse moved into the house meant for Aunt Clara.

Aunt Clara was left to live out her old age in a ramshackle rental house. For a while, Aunt Clara was angry with my mother, until she found out what had happened. Aunt Clara had warned Mama earlier to stay away from her siblings. "They don't mean you no good." Whenever my mother's brothers or sisters and their families were down on their luck, they would come to live either in Big Ma's house or the rental income house, but not pay rent or buy food.

How old was I when I realized that Mama's family was using her? When I was nine I was walking through Central Park with my mother. Mama pointed out the mistletoe growing on a tree and explained that the mistletoe took nutrients from the tree but gave nothing back. My mother said she was like the tree and her family was like the mistletoe; they were parasites.

We never heard from our extended family when the family members were doing well. When they had money, when they had cars, others received the benefits of their good fortune.

I agreed with Mama that it wasn't so much the money that they never paid back, but that they were never there if you needed anything. After I graduated from Yale, I went to Japan to teach English as a Second Language. That first winter I was in Japan, my mother caught the flu. When Mama called her sister, Vera, to let her know she was sick, Vera—even though she came to work in Manhattan every day—said she couldn't stop by because she was afraid of catching it. Not one of my mother's sisters, nieces, or nephews came by to see if she needed a cup of tea or a bowl of soup. A friend heard that Mama was sick and dropped by to make her something to eat.

The people in the street, who used to see my mother pass by every morning on her way to the bus stop to go to work, missed her for a week. One man traced Mama back to her apartment, found out her name, and called up to her window from the street. He wanted to find out if my mother was all right. By then Mama felt better and declined his offer of help.

Chapter 6: Getting the Apartment

Page 119 **I went out on the street:** My mother was using a resource readily available to her, the cop on the beat as a legal advisor. Founded in 1844, with its officers first patrolling in 1845, the New York City Police Department is the oldest municipal police force in the United States.

Page 123 **He told Len to:** My great-grandparents on my father's side were named Leak Jones and Bib Taylor. My aunt on my father's side told me they were Indians from Virginia, most likely Cherokees, "the people." They were given last names by the minister so they could marry.

The 1900 census lists Leak and Bib with one child, who might be my grandfather; they are listed as black. My aunts and uncles on my father's side definitely had Indian features: sharp cheekbones, black wavy hair, and little or no facial hair on the men.

Chapter 7: Creating a Career

Page 137 "**You can stay on:** *Regulating the Poor: the Functions of Public Welfare,* by Frances Fox Piven and Richard Cloward, states that in 1951 the monthly Aid for Families with Dependent Children's average payment in the Northeast was $27 per person per month (132).

Even two years later it probably would not have gone up, since cost-of-living increases were not part of the system. My mother was being asked to quit a $180-a-month position with benefits in a reputable company for a $54-a-month welfare payment.

Page 148 **The school was the:** I was around ten when Mama went to NYID. I was glad she was going, but I was sad, too. One night I sang with the chorus in a program at the school; it was a Thursday night, so Mama couldn't come. Nora and Mrs. Cahan came instead.

At the kitchen table, one school night, I showed my mother and her friends how to study for their midterm.

I helped them organize their notes so they would do well on the test. I thought it was so neat that my mother was going to school at the same time that I was. Mama staked out the kitchen table, while I worked on the dining room table as usual.

When my mother went up to accept her prizes at graduation wearing her white dietitian's uniform, I was happy for her. Mama never received a grade under 90 in food chemistry. Later, in high school, my chemistry grades were nowhere near 90.

Page 155 **I told Francine:** Mama doesn't discuss this, but many people had a difficult time accepting a black woman in a leadership position in a major corporation. Vendors, always white men, would stop by after lunch was over at 2 p.m. to persuade my mother to buy produce or supplies from them for the cafeteria.

All the cafeteria workers wore uniforms. At this time of the day, the staff members, all of whom were black men and women, except for one heavyset white woman, would be behind the counter cleaning up and putting things away in preparation for the next day.

In contrast, my mother, usually wearing a two-piece dress with a jacket, would be seated about three feet from the end of the counter at a desk, with a telephone and an adding machine, doing paperwork.

Invariably, the salesman would approach the white heavyset woman in the uniform cleaning the counter and address her as Mrs. Jones. "No," she would reply, "that's Mrs. Jones at the desk." When Mama told me this story she never said whether or not the vendor was embarrassed about his assumption that the supervisor of the cafeteria had to be overweight and white.

And how did my mother feel about this? I heard a ripple of humor in Mama's voice when she told me this story. Despite the unconscious bias of the salesman, ultimately he had to acknowledge that my mother was in charge.

Vendors weren't the only people who had a hard time accepting Mama as head of the cafeteria. In her years as supervisor, my mother had issues with black men, black women, and white women who could not accept the authority of an African American woman. At one point, a group of black staff members complained to her immediate supervisor about a decision that Mama had made. He told the employees that Mrs. Jones was in charge. If they wanted to stay in their jobs, they would have to abide by her rules, or leave. Those who were the most discontented did leave.

Another aspect of the tragic legacy of European enslavement of African prisoners of war was manifested in the racial composition of the staff itself. When Mama first

375

began working at Standard Brands, under a white female supervisor, she was not only the only black employee in the cafeteria, but also in the company. Eventually, the cafeteria staff became all black.

A few years after Mama became the supervisor, a white woman who worked in the test kitchen revealed that she had wanted to work in the cafeteria because she wanted to create colorful salads.

Meanwhile, a black cafeteria staff member had wanted to work in the test kitchen as a dishwasher, the job that the white woman was given. The personnel department had directed these women to positions that maintained the all-white staff of the test kitchen, with a white supervisor, and the all-black staff of the cafeteria, with a black supervisor. Dissatisfied, they each left their respective jobs.

Chapter 8: Being Involved with Children

Page 184 **My sister, Nora:** After Nora's New York City textile factory job moved to Mexico, she passed the civil- service exam to become a traffic officer, directing street traffic. Mama made an appointment for Nora— when she was ready to give up—at a drivers' education school, so she could pass the driving part of the test. Aunt Nora worked as a traffic officer until she retired.

Page 185 **And those nieces and nephews:** With guidance and exposure, it was easy to see what my mother's nieces and nephews might have accomplished. One cousin designed a multicelled wooden planter for his mother that was both functional and aesthetically pleasing. Another had a beautiful singing voice. And my other cousin, Steve, Vera's middle son, would have made an excellent lawyer.

Chapter 9: Buying the Brownstone

Page 186 **After I graduated:** Since she was still working, my mother told me which bus lines she wanted to be near and the purchase price that she could afford. I read all the papers every day. Even though the Sunday edition of the *Amsterdam News*, established in 1909, one of the oldest black newspapers in the country, was the best place to look, I didn't want to miss anything.

In the summer of 1975, white former students of the Polytechnic Institute of New York were eyeing the brownstones near their Fort Greene campus, but were not interested in Harlem. And the majority of middle-class African Americans were moving to nearby suburbs or New Jersey for better public schools and to escape the drugs that were destroying their young people.

Then it happened. On a Wednesday, I found a listing for 137 West 122 Street in the *New York Times*. Nobody who was serious about selling a brownstone in Harlem in 1975 would put it in the *New York Times*. And nearly all real estate listings were placed in Sunday papers.

The owner's daughter was in her fifties. She had lived in the house since she was five. After she married and had a daughter of her own, she had continued to live there rent-free in return for managing the tenants for her mother. I suspected she did not want the house to be sold. She was the one who had placed the ad.

The house sang to us when we walked through the large wooden door. Most of the stunning woodwork was intact, as well as the stained-glass windows on the parlor floor. The house had twelve rooms and five of the original seven gas-burning fireplaces. I had never seen my mother so happy.

Page 187 **"All right"**: The purchase price was $18,000: $15,000 for the house plus $3,000 for one quarter's taxes. First National City Bank, Citibank's name at the time, my mother's longtime bank, would not write a mortgage on the house.

Although redlining was outlawed by that time, the loan officer openly admitted not giving mortgages in that neighborhood, but said she could return when she needed a loan for home improvement. Mama was prepared for this by her course.

She asked for and received a purchase money mortgage. My mother sent her mortgage payments directly to the owner. She agreed to take the house with Rachel (the owner's daughter) and the sole roomer still in it. The contract gave them a year to move.

Within the year, they had moved.

Page 188 **I want it as a place:** In *Harlem: Lost and Found*, Michael Henry Adams, architectural historian and family friend, details the history of the house in his book on Harlem brownstones. Francis H. Kimball designed the six houses on the block (133, 135, 137, 139, 141, and 143) on 122nd Street, which were built by Italian craftsmen in 1887. Mama's house, no. 137, is in the middle of the set as part of a twin with its next-door neighbor. The two houses share a common middle stair rail.

Brownstones at that time were constructed in groups, with holes between the houses which workmen would walk through to put the same components in each house at the same time. For instance, all the banisters would be put in all the houses on the same day or group of days. Although the artistic elements in each house were similar, no two were exactly alike. The house was built for Mrs. Charles D. Gambrill, widow of the American architect. Mrs. Gambrill could no longer afford her larger house in Brooklyn after the death of her spouse, so she moved to this smaller house.

Kimball was an American architect who supervised American projects for William Burges, the nineteenth-century English architect. He was a pioneer in the use of ornamental terra-cotta and was known as "the father of the skyscraper." Kimball's other still-standing New York buildings include the former residence of Gertrude Rhinelander Waldo (1898), which is now the main Ralph Lauren store at 72nd Street and Madison in Manhattan, and the Montauk Club at Grand Army Plaza in Brooklyn (1891).

My mother was also glad to have the house because it was the fulfillment of a childhood dream. She told Michael Henry Adams about the mansion owned by the Shell family, whose land her family was sharecropping, when he interviewed her for *Harlem: Lost and Found*.

> One of the reasons I have this house today is because of a promise that I made to myself back when I was just a little girl. Our place was down by the river, just on the outside of town. Up on the hill above us the Shells' Victorian mansion stood empty. Old Mrs. Shells was widowed and went to live with her son. The homestead was too big for her. We were crowded in our little cabin. Although allowed to play up there in all twenty rooms,

we couldn't live in the Shells' house—it was considered too good a place for colored to live in. I vowed one day to live in my own mansion (259–60).

Chapter 10: Losing Creativity at Work

No Notes

Chapter 11: This Party's Over

Page 214 **Had I not had:** With advice from Mr. Cahan, Mama sued Nabisco Brands for age discrimination. She had not been asked to go to the relocation site: East Hanover, New Jersey. The company settled out of court.

Chapter 12: Community Work

Page 249 **I bonded with:** Many of these men were retired from the building trades. They lived in one of the brownstones, but had built a cabin-like structure in the courtyard of the adjacent vacant house. This cabin had electrical wiring for their television and some rudimentary furniture so they could watch sports and drink beer together during the summer. It was like a clubhouse. At one point, a reporter wrote an article about the Hale

House, the children's shelter across the street, in which he erroneously described the tree people as homeless.

<u>Page 266</u> **The new people:** The new apartment dwellers did not realize that the buildings they were now living in were only there because Mama and the tree people had prevented them from being demolished. My mother was hurt and angry that the new residents did not appreciate the hard work that she and the others had done to create a clean, drug-free block for them to move into.

Although my mother always relished being the leader, if the newcomers had acknowledged her contribution, she would have—without bitterness—stepped aside for them to take charge of the block association.

<u>Page 266</u> **I will get to the bottom:** Several pieces of mail arrived with my mother's address and the community organization's name. In addition, the head of the organization took pictures of the block cleanup Mama had organized. This led my mother to believe that the organization was claiming the work she and the tree people had done as its own in order to receive grant money.

<u>Page 266</u> **I don't know:** Mama was on the first Mount Morris Park house tour in the mid-nineteen

eighties, which raised funds for the Mount Morris Block Association. Michael Henry Adams, the architectural historian, who later became a family friend, was one of the organizers. He stopped by my mother's house to ask her if she would participate in the tour. She showed him into the back parlor, which was so full of furniture, lamps, china, books, and papers that it looked like a warehouse.

Mama said she would be happy to be on the tour and would let people inside the house. Many of the other participants would only allow people to see the outside of their homes.

"It's a lovely house, Mrs. Jones, but are you sure you're going to be ready in time? The tour is next week."

"Don't worry. I'll get it straightened out."

Michael walked out the door and down the steps sure of my mother's good intentions, but skeptical that she could get the house ready in time for the tour.

When the Sunday afternoon of the tour arrived, not only was the house beautifully arranged, but Mama had also created wonderful refreshments: a fresh fruit platter and cold drinks, which she served in the back parlor. Participants could eat and drink either before or after the tour with her in-house tour guide, me. By this time we had most of the historical information about the house, so I was able to give an informative and enjoyable tour of the house.

Around 1980 we started a brownstoners' group in which owners shared information to help seekers and to help owners who were restoring their homes.

Chapter 13: Working at Olympia & York

<u>Page 278</u> **Citibank was trying:** In 1987 Olympia & York put its own money into Canary Wharf when other investors could not be found. After that, investors joined in the project eagerly, but by 1989 the real estate market bubble had burst, and the company was forced to file for bankruptcy in 1991. By 1995 an international consortium called the Canary Group had taken over management of the site. The wharf is located in the West India Docks on the Isle of Dogs and takes its name from trading with the Canary Islands during its sea trading days.

Chapter 14: Restoring the Brownstone

No Notes

Epilogue: Singing Harlem's Song

No Notes

Appendix: How Mama Nurtured My Education

<u>Page 319</u> **Dalton's holidays and the public school:** Our neighbors weren't the only ones confused by Dalton's different vacation schedule. Columbus Day was a school day for Dalton and a vacation day for the public schools. A driver threw me off his bus for using my bus pass on a holiday. Why the driver thought I would go through the trouble of getting on a bus at 7:30 a.m. with a full book bag on a vacation day just for a free bus ride, I couldn't figure out. I sighed and waited for the next bus. This time I hoped the driver didn't know the public schools were on vacation.

<u>Page 343</u> **The Scholar of the House:** The program started after World War II when the GIs came to Yale. The Scholar of the House Program was for mature students who could work independently. One of the first traditional-age scholars went off to the Caribbean for the school year and didn't complete his project. After that, the program was changed so there was more oversight.

ACKNOWLEDGMENTS

Whenever I give thanks I'm always afraid of missing someone, so first I will thank the people whose names I have mistakenly left out.

Thank you to the late Arlene Lloyd and Claire Parfait for detailed comments on an early version, and to S.L. Jackson for the tenth revision and the gift of the sabbatical. I thank Michael Henry Adams for his helpful advice throughout the writing of this book. Thanks to Juliet L. Gumbs for smoothing out many bumpy patches through her professional close reading of the proof copy. For taking care of our son while I wrote, I express my gratitude to Eddie Ravelo, Lisa Athan, and Natalie Marino. Many thanks for the support the book and I have received from all the people who assist me in taking care of my mother: Josephine Israel, Paulette Laurent, Nicole Burns, Enide Jerome, Ruth Ismael, Utilia Dormeus, Oparo Okwudiri, Monique Hodge, Gina Lewis, Rose Beaujuin, Desreen Calvert, Angela Woods, Elizabeth Bonadventura, Andrew Siscock, Tara Spillane, and anyone that I have left out. Eric Lerner read serial drafts of the book proposal, and

Enid Goldberg attempted to get the book into the world; I thank both of you. Thanks to all of you for your sistership, brothership, and friendship.

I am grateful to Unity of Montclair members, not only for spiritual support, but also for a series of *Poets' Night* events. These readings, wonderfully co-organized and originally initiated by my co-chair, Paula Thomas, and masterfully presented by Les Henson, allowed me to connect with my audience and receive an immediate response. I give thanks to Gretna Wilkinson, Paul Corley, the Reading Group, Denise Lewis Patrick, Austin Patrick, Sarah Henseler, Roz Jones, Chrysoula Fantaousakis, Sue Tegge, and the Springfield Library Book Club for sistership, brothership, friendship, and spiritual support.

I am deeply indebted to everyone in the traditional publishing industry who read the manuscript, in whole or in part, and offered their opinions. Whether I agreed with them or not, they all led me in the right direction. To the last publisher who said no and the two publishers after that whose submission guidelines included questions or conditions that made it clear that Ida Bell Publishing, LLC, was the answer, I say thank you. For excellent guidance, I thank *The Complete Guide to Self-Publishing* by Marilyn Ross and Sue Collier.

And now for the physical book. I give warm thanks to all my creative colleagues in book editing and production who are listed by name and title in the front of the book, but I want to give them specific thanks here. Thanks to Frank Steele, whose transformation of that worrisome sentence was only the beginning of the miracle of his copyediting, fact checking, proofreading, and excellent book production information, for which I will always be grateful. Thank you to Natalie Marino for the fun I had sharing the sparks that fly off her visual mind, her work on the photos, her stunning cover, and all her consulting advice. Denise DeVone reminded me to look for the negatives, produced the scans of my mother's superb culinary art so her work could be reproduced with the highest quality photos and did imaginative work on the fundraising video. I thank the late Sharon Gayle for her sharp editing of an earlier version and for the life's lessons she taught me. Anita Diggs, my current editor, made sure the book retained its heart center and did it with great humor and integrity. Mark Pollachek's fine tax advice not only placed the manuscript onto the first step in book production, but also ensured that Ida Bell Publishing, LLC, was in compliance with IRS regulations. Thanks to BookBaby and NextWave Web and all your staff members for being so helpful to a first-time publisher. Yes, the craft of book production is a delightful collaboration, but I am solely responsible for all mistakes or omissions.

Without my family and their endurance during this long gestation, this book wouldn't exist. I am boundlessly grateful to my mother, Josephine E. Jones, for having the courage to tell her story and the kindness to trust me with it. I thank our son, Hiroshi, for being an early reader of the book. Many thanks to my life partner, David Mitchell, for invaluable technical assistance, and for being a hands-on father, a loving partner, and a Renaissance man.

And lastly, I thank the Universe for co-creating with me.

LIST OF SPONSORS

Thank You for Your Generous Contributions

Nina Beaty

Faith Brancato

Ted Brancato

Paul Corley

Richard Friedhoff

Kim Heilig

Sarah Henseler

Les Henson

S.L. Jackson

Lisa Lewis-Neal

Matthew MacDonald

Carolyn Malloy

Hillary Mitchell

Robin Mitchell

Claire Parfait

Jane Rosenman

Barbara Russo

Nina Smith

Hisao Tateishi

Tynia Thomassie

Carol Vasquez

Gretna Wilkinson

BIBLIOGRAPHY

Adams, Michael Henry. *Harlem: Lost and Found.* New York: The Monacelli Press, 2002.

Anderson, James D. *The Education of Blacks in the South, 1860–1935.* Chapel Hill, NC: University of North Carolina Press, 1988.

Blackmon, Douglas A. *Slavery by Another Name: The Re-Enslavement of Black Americans from the Civil War to World War II.* New York: Doubleday, 2008.

Cook, Blanche Wiesen. *Eleanor Roosevelt, Volume Two (1933–1938).* New York: Viking Press, 1999.

Cox, Jim. *Sold on Radio: Advertisers in the Golden Age of Broadcasting.* Jefferson, NC: McFarland & Company, 2008.

Foner, Eric. *Reconstruction: America's Unfinished Revolution.* New York: Perennial Classics, 2002.

Hodgson, Godfrey. *The Gentleman from New York: Daniel Patrick Moynihan: A Biography.* Boston: Houghton Mifflin, 2000.

Marable, Manning. *Malcolm X: A Life of Reinvention.* New York: Viking, 2011.

Piven, Frances Fox, and Richard Cloward. *Regulating the Poor: The Functions of Public Welfare.* New York: Pantheon, 1971.

Shilts, Randy. *And the Band Played On.* New York: Penguin Books, 1988.

Terborg-Penn, Rosalyn. *African American Women in the Struggle for the Vote, 1850–1920.* Bloomington: Indiana University Press, 1998.

Wilkerson, Isabel. *The Warmth of Other Suns.* New York: Random House, 2010.

Wilkes, Paul and Joy. *You Don't Have to Be Rich to Own a Brownstone.* New York: Quadrangle/New York Times, 1973.

For background on Olympia and York, see Anthony Bianco, *The Reichmanns: Family, Faith, Fortune, and the Empire of Olympia & York* (New York: Times Business, 1997).

Thanks to Jay Jung of the Korea Society in New York for his Korean transliteration.

And special thanks to Theodore Rosengarten for *All God's Dangers.*

For me, he started it all.

LIST OF PHOTOS

AFTER CHAPTER 4: FAMILY

1. Big Pa

2. Big Ma

3. Len Jones

4. Early Days at Standard Brands

AFTER CHAPTER 7: CULINARY ART

5. Crenshaw Melon

6. Fruit Bowl

7. Apple Birds

8. Ham with Rice and Chaudfroid Sauce

9. Sandwiches with Vegetables

10. Gelatin and Cake

11. Shrimp with Dipping Sauce

12. Not-a-Cake Sandwich Loaf

13. Vegetable Salad Fixings

14. Pineapple with Honeydew and Watermelon

AFTER CHAPTER 11: EVERYTHING ELSE

ABOUT THE AUTHOR

Wendy Jones is an author, playwright, and the writer-publisher of **Ida Bell Publishing, LLC**. Named after Ida B. Wells, the writer and social activist, the company will publish the work of people of color, new immigrants, all women, and other outsiders.

Her first play, *In Pursuit of Justice: A One-Woman Play about Ida B. Wells*, which starred Janice Jenkins, won four **AUDELCO** Awards. Her writing has appeared in two anthologies: *Streetlights: Illuminating Tales of the Urban Black Experience*, and *The Point: Where Teaching & Writing Intersect*. She is the fiction editor of theravensperch.com, an online literary magazine.

As president of **Writing Maven, LLC**, she helps people write essays, resumes, and wedding vows and prepares students for the SAT and the ACT. She is a former tenured English professor.

She lives in New Jersey with her life partner, David Mitchell, and their son.